UNDERSTANDABLE ECONOMICS

Because Understanding Our Economy Is Easier Than You Think and More Important Than You Know

Howard Yaruss

Prometheus Books

Essex, Connecticut

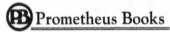 **Prometheus Books**

An imprint of Globe Pequot, the trade division of
The Rowman & Littlefield Publishing Group, Inc.
4501 Forbes Blvd., Ste. 200
Lanham, MD 20706
www.rowman.com

Distributed by NATIONAL BOOK NETWORK

British Library Cataloguing in Publication Information Available

Library of Congress Cataloging-in-Publication Data
Name: Yaruss, Howard, 1958–. author.
Title: Understandable economics : because understanding our economy is easier than
    you think and more important than you know / Howard Yaruss.
Description: Lanham, MD : Rowman & Littlefield, 2022. | Includes index. | Summary:
    "This essential and engaging guide provides readers with a practical understanding
    of our economy and the ability to identify, understand, and advocate for constructive
    solutions to the problems we face"—Provided by publisher.
Identifiers: LCCN 2022001233 (print) | LCCN 2022001234 (ebook) | ISBN
    9781633888364 (cloth) | ISBN 9781633888371 (epub)
Subjects: LCSH: Economics. | Business cycles. | Finance. | Economic policy.
Classification: LCC HB171.5 .Y37 2022 (print) | LCC HB171.5 (ebook) | DDC
    330—dc23/eng/20220111
LC record available at https://lccn.loc.gov/2022001233
LC ebook record available at https://lccn.loc.gov/2022001234

For David,
who makes the ordinary seem extraordinary
and the truly extraordinary seem possible.

CONTENTS

PREFACE

If you can't explain it simply, you don't understand it well enough.

—Albert Einstein

Although many economists are reluctant to admit it, economics is not a scientific discipline that requires expert knowledge and specialized tools to gain understanding. It's not like biology, where you need to know organic chemistry and have access to a microscope and other equipment to know what's going on in living cells. It's not like astrophysics, where you need to know the relationships among the forces in the universe and have access to powerful telescopes to figure out the properties of a black hole.

Like psychology, economics is a social science, an attempt to understand human interactions and how they affect the world around us. It focuses on those relationships as they relate to money as well as the goods, services, and resources money buys. In order to tease out some precision regarding those relationships, professional economists use data and mathematical tools. But the fundamental relationships themselves will become apparent if you're willing to observe the world carefully and apply your own common sense. The goal of this book is to help you do that.

I'm not going to tell you what or how to think—there is no shortage of authors, pundits, influencers, and Twitter celebrities happy to do that. My aim is to demystify our economy by engaging with it in a direct, practical, and (I hope) entertaining manner. I want you to be able to think through these issues for yourself and draw your own conclusions. Not all of our conclusions will be the same, but the objectives are that they will all be based on how the world actually works and provide insight into what policies could meaningfully improve our economic well-being.

I'm sure many of you have wondered about the following:

- Why is economic inequality soaring, and what can we do about it?
- Is there an alternative to capitalism that will solve more problems than it creates?
- Why do the green slips of paper in our wallets and Bitcoin have value?
- Could alternative currencies replace the dollar?
- Do tax cuts for the wealthy create jobs or just more inequality?
- Why do so many people believe free trade is good if some people lose jobs as a result?
- How can we influence the behavior of corporations?
- Why does the economy regularly turn down and how can we get it back on track?
- What is the Federal Reserve System, and how does it affect us?
- Is our national debt too big, and should it limit future government spending?
- What policies would help grow the economy?

Understandable Economics provides necessary background information and discusses what's going on in the real world so you can respond to questions such as these with insight and confidence.

This may be your first attempt to understand what drives our economy, since most Americans never take a course in economics. Those of you who have taken an economics course were probably confronted with a bewildering array of jargon, formulas, graphs, and assumptions that seem to have little connection to reality, leaving you with a limited understanding, at best, of these issues. Most books on the subject take the same dry, technical approach, quickly sapping the interest of all but the most determined readers.

I know this because I was one of the determined ones who studied economics and slogged through many courses and countless books on the subject. Why was I so determined? I grew up in Brooklyn in a family that often faced financial difficulties. I started working in my early teens and spent a good part of my time as a young adult helping my father in his grocery store. I became painfully aware of the great disparities in education, security, material well-being, and opportunity. I saw how these inequalities caused some people to become cynical, resigned, or indifferent—while others became determined to overcome them. I became fascinated by them. I felt that if I wanted to live in a more just and productive society, I first had to understand how it worked. I believe the same is true for you.

I want you to be able to identify better solutions for the problems we face so you are not dependent on others for direction. I want you to be able to assess which politicians are proposing policies that would grow our economy and provide more opportunity. I want you to be able to advocate for solutions with the confidence that an understanding of the economic system brings. I want you to feel empowered to defend those solutions against the inaccurate criticisms so prevalent in social-media echo chambers.

The need for this understanding is more important now than ever. The belief that our economic system is failing is at a record high, and for good reason. Incomes are stagnating, middle-class jobs are disappearing, the economy is growing more slowly, and the meager gains produced are almost exclusively going to those

who are already wealthy. There has been a wide range of reactions
to these economic changes, from Occupy Wall Street to the election of Donald Trump. What is the one thing all of these reactions
have in common? They have not resulted in any significant positive change in the lives of most Americans.

This book seeks to change that. I believe that if more of us were
armed with a better understanding of how the economy works,
more constructive solutions for the problems we face would be
implemented and we would finally see the economy improve
for the average person. Whether your own goal is to change the
world, to better evaluate candidates for public office, or simply to
be better informed, my hope is that this book will help you assess
what is possible and inspire you to make our nation more equitable and productive.

As people often correctly say, democracy is not a spectator
sport. Its health depends upon the participation of well-informed
people like yourself.

Part I

THE ECONOMIC SYSTEM

1

CAPITALISM

What Gets Made, and Who Gets What?

The inherent vice of capitalism is the unequal sharing of blessings; the inherent virtue of socialism is the equal sharing of miseries.

—Winston Churchill

CAPITALISM, SOCIALISM, OTHER "ISMS," AND REALITY

What do Helen Keller, Adolph Hitler, Oscar Wilde, Joseph Stalin, and Nelson Mandela have in common? They all called themselves "socialists." Meanwhile, former president Donald Trump, who broke all conventions and radically departed from the status quo, is called "conservative"; people who fault the media for not sticking to the truth are called "liberal"; and sycophants who make a living by cozying up to politicians are called "capitalists." Clearly, many of the key terms used to describe economic and political systems have lost their meanings. Labels like "capitalist" and "socialist" have become so distorted and politicized over time that they serve more often as insults than as a succinct and accurate summary of someone's worldview. Therefore, they aren't particularly useful in helping us to look fairly and objectively at our economic system and gain insight into how it actually works.

In order to start understanding the economy, we need to begin with the most fundamental economic questions: Who gets what? and Who does what? Today, with so much stuff to allocate (such as cars, phones, college educations, and books on economics) and so many things to do (such as building cars, assembling phones, teaching, and writing books on economics), countless decisions have to be made. How can we make these decisions?

On one hand, these decisions could be made collectively by the government. In this scenario, the government owns everything and makes all the decisions. It decides how much food to produce (and who produces it) and how much coal to mine (and who mines it). It decides who gets the mansion on the coast and who gets stuck with a cramped apartment near the factory. Karl Marx wrote about this collectivist system, which is often summed up as "from each according to his ability, to each according to his needs." This system is similar to "communism" and "Marxism," as defined in textbooks.

On the other hand, these decisions could be made individually. In this scenario, everything is privately owned. Each person is free to do whatever they want with their time and resources. Clearly, these decisions are linked, since what you choose to do with your time greatly affects how much you can afford to buy and vice versa. But the government has no, or a very limited, role in these decisions. In the extreme version of this system, government doesn't even exist. In the less extreme version, the government has a limited ability to intervene if your actions cause direct harm—like if you pollute the environment, make hazardous products, or decide to practice medicine with no medical knowledge. This system is similar to "libertarianism" and "laissez-faire" (French for "let it be"), as defined in textbooks.

You can think of all economic systems that actually exist in the real world as being located somewhere along a spectrum between these two extremes—where decisions are made collectively (on the left side) to where decisions are made individually (on the right side). So, what kind of economic system is "capitalism"?

The textbook definition of "capitalism" is an economic system where businesses (the means of production) are owned and managed by private individuals, rather than collectively by the government. The United States and most Western nations are often called capitalist, yet they fail to meet this definition since their businesses fall far short of being truly "owned and managed" privately. These nations regulate how, what, where, and by whom products are produced; serve as a partner in every business through the income tax system; directly produce and provide a variety of goods and services from education to housing to food; decide whether businesses can merge with or acquire their competitors; and control how employees can be treated and paid. Any system that permits completely free and unfettered private control of business and fully meets the textbook definition of "capitalism" would lack the ability to protect consumers from being cheated, the environment from harm, and workers from being exploited. It could not be successful in the real world.

Conversely, every "communist" nation, including North Korea, has some private enterprise and therefore meets the definition of capitalism to some extent. In particular, "Communist" China has innumerable entrepreneurs, some of whom have become multi-billionaires by building successful businesses. Why do all nations have at least some form of private enterprise? If the government owned and controlled all production, it would have to figure out what each person needed, how to produce all of it, and what each person's contribution to that production would be. Furthermore, in a system where the "needs" of all people are met, regardless of what they do or don't do for work, motivating each person to do all the tasks necessary to make that possible would be difficult, to say the least. The level of government control in such a system and the ethical and logistical issues of getting everyone to do what the government needed them to do are unimaginable. It would be just as unworkable as a system in which there is no role for government and collective action.

Therefore, what we have in the real world today is a hybrid system. On one hand, businesses in the vast majority of nations are rarely owned and controlled by the government. On the other hand, the legal system and the government's countless rules, restrictions, and incentives greatly influence what businesses produce and how they produce it.

Similarly, the government doesn't tell individual people what their role in the economy will be. Nevertheless, most people don't have unlimited options. The great variation in educational quality and the expense of higher education certainly limit many people's choices and take a huge toll on economic opportunity, as we will discuss in future chapters. Furthermore, individual state licensing requirements, such as those for florists, interior designers, casket salespeople, and salon shampooers, also restrict choice (and often seem more focused on protecting people in certain professions from competition than on protecting the public). Add to that employer biases, the difficulty of relocating, and the declining number of employers, and we seem far from the ideal that each person's role in the economy is the result of a truly free choice.

As a practical matter, the term "capitalism" is usually used and is used in this book to simply refer to this hybrid economic system as it actually exists in the United States and most nations today. Some economic decisions are made collectively by the government; some are made individually; and many result from the interaction between the individual and the government. "Socialism" generally refers to a system with more regulation and collective control, and "conservatism" generally refers to a system with less regulation and collective control.

We can continue this philosophical discussion and get further into the meaning of the term "capitalism," along with the terms "socialism," "conservatism," "libertarianism," "communism," "Marxism," and all of the other "isms," but we won't. Each of those terms is fraught with so many assumptions, associations, and preconceived ideas that focusing on them may in fact obstruct our goal—to understand how the real world works, what specific problems exist, and how those problems can be addressed.

When people express an opinion on or a dissatisfaction with "capitalism," I assume they are commenting on the economic system as it actually exists in the world today and not some system that exists in a theoretical model. Therefore, in order to address any issues people raise regarding our economic system, we first need to find the right balance between collective control through government action and individual control through private choice. That balance should depend on what would produce the best outcome, rather than what would fit into some particular ideological framework.

Hundreds of years of trial and error have resulted in the mixed economic system we have today. Lately, however, more people have been expressing concern about the outcomes this system is producing. The middle class is being squeezed and the economy is growing more slowly, while the wealthy are doing better than ever. We are not headed in the best direction. But before we can assess where we are headed, we need some perspective on where we have come from.

ECONOMIC GROWTH AND THE INDUSTRIAL REVOLUTION

The argument for limiting government involvement in business is that businesses will naturally seek to produce what people most want. Why? Because that will earn them the greatest sales and, therefore, the greatest profit. This is what Adam Smith, one of the founders of modern economics, was talking about in 1776 when he wrote, "It is not from the benevolence of the butcher, the brewer, or the baker that we expect our dinner, but from their regard to their own interest." Smith believed that the incentive to earn a profit resulted in an "invisible hand" that would direct each business, more effectively than any government officials could, to provide the most desired goods and services.

In the late 1700s in England, this process kicked into high gear because the advent of steam power and other innovations enabled mechanized, factory production to replace much less efficient production by hand. This "Industrial Revolution" transformed the way most goods could be manufactured. The freedom many people had to start their own businesses caused these innovations to spread far and wide. Any industry slow to take advantage of these advances would present a great business opportunity for others. Entrepreneurs could set up new, more efficient operations and put their competitors who clung to the old methods of production out of business. This process—whereby more-efficient producers drive out less-efficient ones—is often called "creative destruction."

Adam Smith gave a classic example of this shift from individual production by hand to what we would today call assembly-line production in a factory. He wrote about how one worker would have a difficult time producing one pin in a day, but ten workers in a factory that divided up the manufacture of a pin into several distinct operations could produce about 48,000 pins in a day. I am not sure about the accuracy of his exact number, but I am sure about his point: that the division of labor, specialization, and mass production can radically increase output.

Often overlooked in the story of industrialization is that prior to this revolution, the vast majority of people were desperately poor. In particular, for almost all of human history prior to the last couple of hundred years, most people had few possessions, lived much shorter and less healthy lives, and often faced hunger or worse. That was because production methods rarely improved prior to the Industrial Revolution. For example, if you look at how a shoe was made in ancient Rome, how it was made a thousand years later in medieval Europe, and how it was made in the Renaissance just prior to the Industrial Revolution, you wouldn't see much change. Cobblers, like almost every other worker, pretty much used the same tools in the same way with the same materials for almost all of human history. Since the amount each cobbler and each other worker could produce barely changed, for one person to have more, some other person needed to have less. The economy was essentially a zero-sum game.

The Industrial Revolution changed all of that. It ushered in constantly improving efficiencies in production that allowed industrialized economies to turn out goods at a rate that was inconceivable before that time. Nevertheless, life in the early factories was miserable; it was probably the worst conditions people who were not expressly being punished or enslaved had ever endured. The hours were excessive, the environment was filthy and unsafe, the pay was poor, and the whole experience would be inconceivable and intolerable to workers in the United States and other advanced nations today. Work in the early factories may have provided people with a modestly higher income and food security, but often at the cost of a wretched and shortened life.

Writing in the mid-1800s, as the Industrial Revolution was coming into full swing, Karl Marx despaired about the conditions wrought by industrialization. He predicted that the misery imposed on workers by the factory owners (the "capitalists") would eventually result in a "proletarian revolution" and a government takeover of all business. His revolution hasn't happened yet and a government takeover of all business doesn't seem to be anywhere on the horizon. Why not?

As the amount of output each worker produced soared, more and more goods were unloaded onto the market, causing prices to fall. When Adam Smith's pre-industrial pin makers took a full day to make their pins, pins were scarce and expensive. As soon as ten of them got together in a factory and started producing 48,000 a day, there was such an abundance of pins that the price had to plummet to get people to buy them all. This reduced price was not like the reduced price of corn in a year with a particularly good harvest. The cost of producing pins and all sorts of other goods had permanently plummeted, and the higher pre–Industrial Revolution prices became a thing of the past.

If a factory owner tried to rip off consumers and charge something close to the old higher prices, they would lose their customers to an enterprising new factory owner. Capitalism ensured that producers of goods shared some of the vast cost savings from factory production with consumers—if they didn't, their new competitor would.

Lower prices and greater output meant that the average person was eventually able to purchase significantly more goods and enjoy a higher standard of living. The Federal Reserve Bank of Dallas provided a great indication of how much better off people have become by calculating how many minutes an average American worker would need to work to purchase various basic goods. From 1919 (when our nation was still in the process of industrializing) to 1997, the "cost" in terms of minutes of paid labor a worker would need to perform fell from 39 minutes to 7 minutes for a half gallon of milk, from 30 minutes to 6 minutes for a pound of ground beef, and from 9.5 hours to 1.6 hours for a sample of a dozen food staples.[1]

Greater productivity (in other words, more output per worker) not only enabled everyone to have more, but also gave them access to an ever-increasing array of products. Improving technology resulted in an explosion of new products and industries, from communications, to motor vehicles, to electric appliances, many of which would have been unimaginable prior to the Industrial Revolution. Many of these, in turn, improved productivity even further.

Just as capitalism pushed the prices of goods down, so too did it eventually push wages up. If a business owner tried to keep wages low as the economy was growing, workers could seek employment elsewhere. If business owners as a whole were slow to raise wages and earned obscene profits at the expense of their workers, the market was full of eager entrepreneurs who could set up a competing business and attract workers by offering higher pay while still earning a good profit, albeit not an obscene one.

The ability of workers to jump ship and get higher wages elsewhere led Henry Ford to double his motor company's wages for employees early in the twentieth century. He noticed his business was experiencing high turnover, losing workers who were very expensive to train. Many people incorrectly think Ford increased wages to enable his workers to afford to buy his cars and thereby increase his profits. That conclusion sounds nice, but simple arithmetic proves it wrong. The additional money Ford paid his employees was certain to be spent on a wide range of goods and services, not just new Ford cars.[2] Furthermore, only a portion of any money that these higher-paid workers spent on Ford cars was profit for Ford, since a large portion of the price paid for a new car goes to the cost of manufacturing the car. The moral of this story? Even Henry Ford, one of the largest and most powerful industrialists of all time, succumbed to market pressures to raise wages.

This, of course, was not true in all cases. The most glaring example: Enslaved people were, to say the least, far from free to seek better opportunities both before the Civil War and in many cases after. Even today, as we discussed in the last section, most people don't have unlimited options regarding what they do with their lives. Nevertheless, people's freedom to choose their own destiny has grown significantly over time and, although we have much further to go, we have greatly expanded individual opportunity and benefitted from the economic growth it enables.

Today, a person in an average job in the United States can enjoy a greater diversity and quality of food, access a wider variety of entertainment, live longer with good health, and, in general, lead a much better life than even the most privileged could before the industrial era. I was reminded of how much life has improved in the last few hundred years while stopping for lunch along the New Jersey Turnpike. For $15, I was able to eat as much as I wanted from a buffet that included an array of hot foods, salads, cheese, fruits, cakes, and, most importantly, soft-serve ice cream. Modern

farming, transportation, and refrigeration has made all this possible. What would have been an inconceivable feast to even the
wealthiest person before the Industrial Revolution has become
something very ordinary for most of us.

Lower-priced goods, higher wages, and an array of new products led people to expect that their lives would be better than it
was for those who preceded them. In general, they were right.
Most people no longer had to worry about where their next meal
was coming from (it was in the refrigerator) and could instead
turn their attention to improving their lives, their society, and
their working conditions. The number of hours American workers
worked per week dropped from 58.5 hours in 1900[3] to 34.0 hours
in 2020.[4] Workers started forming unions, which played a major
role in raising wages and improving working conditions. They
also had the time and resources to pressure their government to
improve work life. Laws prohibiting child labor, mandating minimum wages, and requiring safe working conditions all followed.

Increasing prosperity thereby created more prosperity in a
virtuous circle. Public education, better sanitary conditions, and
countless improvements in public welfare became affordable and
made the economy even more productive. People could finally
afford to save some of their earnings, providing the funds for
further investment and innovation in business and higher levels
of education for their children. As people became more productive and invested, they not only improved their own lives, but also
improved the entire society.

People often talk about the Agricultural Revolution (which
changed our nation from one dominated by small farmers to one
where less than 2 percent of workers are employed on farms[5])
and the Technological Revolution (which inserted advanced technology into almost everything) as if they are separate and apart
from the Industrial Revolution. They aren't. The focus may have
shifted from manufactured goods, to food, to information and
services, but they are a continuation of the process of rethinking

production to radically increase output that began over two hundred years ago.

Whether we will one day reach a limit to growth in our economy's output is uncertain. What is certain is that ever since the beginning of the Industrial Revolution, the economy, on average, has grown. How much? In the last seventy years, our nation's total output of goods and services* (in other words, stuff) has grown by approximately 2 percent per person per year.[6] Two percent may not sound like much, but it means that the stuff enjoyed by the average American has doubled every thirty-five years. This growth in output and the way much of it has become widely shared would have given Karl Marx and his contemporaries quite a jolt, probably causing them to rethink their prediction of a groundswell of support for a government takeover of the economy and business.

Nevertheless, a recent Gallup poll found that the percentage of Americans with a positive view of capitalism has been steadily dropping.[7] In 2018, only 56 percent of Americans had a positive view of capitalism. Among 18- to 29-year-olds, that number dropped to 45 percent. In 2020, a major poll found that the majority of respondents believed that capitalism in its current form is doing more harm than good in the world.[8] Other polls have had similar results. This increasing disillusionment with capitalism comes, paradoxically, after many decades of significant economic growth in America and the collapse of the more centrally planned "socialist" economies in the Soviet Union and Eastern Europe. So, what has caused this shift? The next chapter seeks to answer that question.

---

* This is the gross domestic product and is discussed in detail in chapter 4.

2

THE CHANGING ECONOMY

Why Are Some People Losing Faith in Our Economic System?

An imbalance between rich and poor is the oldest and most fatal ailment of all republics.

—Plutarch, ancient Greek philosopher

HOW IS CAPITALISM CHANGING?

No matter how good an economic system may be, there will always be shortcomings, disappointments, and room for improvement. No one book could possibly address them all. My goal is to identify the criticisms that are so significant that they are causing people to lose faith in our own economic system and question its legitimacy.

Economics studies the production and distribution of goods and services. Therefore, every economic system is designed to answer: (1) how products are made, (2) what products are made, and (3) who gets what. How our system is answering these three questions has started to cause trouble.

How Products Are Made

Every nation has at least some rules regarding how products are made, such as rules that protect workers in the production process, limit harm to the environment, and prevent consumers from being cheated or injured. They also usually have rules that encourage the production of certain products, like price supports for agriculture and subsidies for solar power, and discourage or prohibit certain other products, like carbon taxes or bans on most opioids.

The need for some regulation of production is clear if you think of the economy as a highway. A few simple rules enable cars to travel efficiently from one place to another. Imagine, however, driving on the highway without speed limits, with a drunk driver on your left and a 10-year-old driver on your right. Now imagine half the cars surrounding you are traveling in the opposite direction that you're going. Sound like a nightmare? Without rules, the highway couldn't function. Similarly, if you were left wondering whether everything you bought would injure you, poison the environment, or work as expected, the economy couldn't function either.

Are the rules we have for how products are made too permissive? Many think they are. Are these rules too strict? Many think they are. The answer plays out through the political process.

The obvious question is: Does our political process fairly represent the wishes of most Americans? The answer: Money has a loud voice in our politics, and current trends are amplifying it even more. As we'll discuss in chapter 8, the U.S. Supreme Court has put the lobbying process on steroids by clearing the way for unlimited cash to flow from corporations to politicians. As a result, auto makers have gotten reduced fuel-efficiency standards, for-profit colleges have gotten more government assistance, farmers have gotten more subsidies, and all of corporate America has gotten massive tax breaks.

Should we expect corporations to simply stop advocating for rules that benefit them? Clearly not, since there's no sign (nor has there ever been a sign) of that happening. In fact, many corporate executives are actually convinced that their advocacy is motivated by a greater good (such as a more productive economy) rather than selfishness, thereby emboldening them to promote their agendas even more aggressively.

These executives often have direct access to the government regulators who decide what policies and procedures get adopted and how, and if, they are enforced. Company executives not only frequently meet with their regulators, but also dine with them, golf with them, and enjoy all sorts of other activities that a huge expense account makes possible. Input from the public, on the other hand, is usually limited to comments, complaints, and letters, which often land on the desks of the lowest-level staffers.

I can say from personal experience as the former general counsel of a large and heavily regulated company, that many regulators begin to identify with the corporate executives with whom they frequently chat. They come to view them (and the politicians supported by them) as their constituency rather than the general public. Regulators have nowhere near the same quality or quantity of contact with the average person—the taxpayers who pay their salaries. These cozy relationships between the regulators and the regulated have the potential to turn into much more highly compensated new jobs for regulators after they leave government later in their careers, making regulators even more receptive to corporate interests. They may be making decisions today that benefit companies they may be seeking to work for tomorrow. "Regulatory capture" is the name of this all-too-common phenomenon in which regulators identify more with those they regulate than with the public they are paid to protect.

If we truly want a regulatory system that pushes businesses to be more responsive to our concerns regarding how products are made, we must act in our own interest, rather than hope that special interests decide one day to do it for us. We need to support politicians who identify specific goals for businesses, such as having less of an impact on the environment, paying the lowest-paid workers something closer to a living wage, or adhering to higher standards in dealing with customers.

The problem is not with capitalism itself. Harmful actions by businesses will exist in any system where people can't or don't assert their demands for how businesses function and workers are treated. In particular, nations with freer markets (in other words, nations with less government control over business, like the United States) often provide more protection from harm for consumers and workers than nations where there is more government control (like China).[1] This may be because people are less able to assert their demands in nations that have a lot of government control over the economy, markets, the press, and most other things. The question of how people in our economic system can more effectively assert themselves and influence business will be discussed in chapter 8.

What Products Are Made

You or I may think that much (most?) of what gets bought and sold in today's economy is wasteful and pointless. But since every one of those goods and services is willingly bought, we know each one has a value to someone that's at least as great as its price. If not, they wouldn't have bought it in the first place.*

For example, there are some people (myself not among them) who would pay $500,000 for a Rolls-Royce Phantom Sedan. Why? Because the satisfaction they would get from owning the car (and, presumably, from seeing other people's reaction to their owning the car) makes the price worthwhile to them. Is there something wrong with that?

On one hand, since we live in a society that values (or says it values) individual freedom, expression, and unfettered choice as

---

* This is also true, in theory at least, of government purchases. Our government representatives authorize the purchase of goods and if we believe what they pay exceeds the value we receive, presumably we would vote them out of office.

long as no one else is harmed, would we be justified in having an objection to a purchase based on such "taste" in cars? And if we did allow such objections to prevent people from buying things, the Rolls-Royce Phantom Sedan purchasers might object to my Toyota Corolla (or, more likely, my bike-share membership).

On the other hand, since what gets produced is what people purchase, significant income inequality means that the whims of some get met while the critical needs of others don't. This is just one of the problems caused by growing income inequality, which is the subject of the next few sections and, to a great extent, a recurring theme in this book.

Who Gets What

In virtually all systems today, how much someone gets is based upon how much money they or their spouse, parent, or some other generous person earns or has earned. And many people view how much someone earns as based on their effort and ability. The harder they work and the smarter they are, the more they are expected to earn.

Many factors other than hard work and smarts, such as being in the right place at the right time or being born into a functional family that lives in a desirable neighborhood with good schools, play a larger role in determining incomes than most people would like to admit. Nevertheless, most people accept that people earn unequal incomes not because it's somehow morally or objectively justified, but simply because it provides a strong incentive for people to be more productive. The thinking goes that if everyone earned the same thing (or very close to it), they wouldn't be motivated to show up for work and, if they were required to show up, they wouldn't be motivated to do much once they got there. Everyone would be equal, but they would all be equally poor because not much would get produced.

If industriousness is rewarded with higher incomes, there is an incentive to work harder and be more productive, resulting in more output to go around for everyone. The Industrial Revolution and its great increase in output and average living standards is often seen as proof that economic incentives work. But more recently, that seems less and less true. Why? Because at some point, growing income inequality, such as we are now experiencing, starts to shrink economic output, rather than add to it. How can that be?

When incomes are more equal, patterns of spending are more regular and consistent. One thousand households, each earning $60,000 a year, are likely to spend almost all of their income (rather than save much of it) and are also likely to spend it in similar ways. They will divide their income in more or less the same way among housing, food, transportation, clothing, utilities, and other basic expenditures. Because these households wind up spending almost all of their combined $60 million in income, almost $60 million of goods and services are produced, creating opportunities and jobs for the many people needed to produce all those goods and services. Furthermore, their somewhat similar and predictable spending habits allow for better, easier, and more efficient planning for production.

On the other hand, if the $60 million in income is split very unevenly among the thousand households, total spending drops and the spending that does occur tends to be more erratic. Why? Higher-income people spend a smaller portion of their earnings (in other words, they save more) than lower-income people. Therefore, less income is plowed back into the economy as spending, less output is produced, and fewer jobs and opportunities are created for others.

Additionally, the spending patterns of high earners tend to be much less predictable. If one household earns fifty times as much as another household, it doesn't buy fifty times as many groceries, cars, and haircuts. What it does with the extra income is anyone's guess. It may be used to purchase a yacht once every decade, have extensive cosmetic surgery, throw a $3 million birthday party (as rapper P. Diddy Combs reportedly did), or pay $69 million for a digital file from one artist (Beeple) while most other artists struggle to keep a roof over their heads.

The chance to earn more than your neighbor (or even more than all of your neighbors combined) does generally incentivize people to work harder and be more productive. But at some point, that incentive wears off. Would Mark Zuckerberg, Bill Gates, or Jeff Bezos not have bothered with Facebook, Microsoft, or Amazon if their taxes were higher, even significantly so? Probably not. My suspicion is that they were so obsessed with their projects that they were not thinking about potential tax rates. And even if each of these three people decided not to set up their company because they feared that the tax on their profits would be too high, would there be no other competent person interested in setting up a social media company, a software provider, or an online retailer? Again, probably not.

Significant inequality shrinks the economic pie (in other words, the total amount of goods and services) for everyone. Even the "winners" in such an economy aren't winning as much as they could—although their share of the economic pie is growing, the total pie is not as big as it could be. For the rest of us, the effects are much worse. Even though many of us are doing fine economically (which, by historical standards, we are), people judge their circumstances subjectively by looking around them. Huge disparities in income, therefore, have the potential to fan the flames of resentment, making people feel that our economic system is unfair and undermining their faith in it.

This is particularly true since people's economic circumstances are increasingly determined by what family they happen to be born into, rather than by what they do. In the United States, approximately 60 percent of all wealth is inherited, meaning that the majority of America's riches, and the many advantages that go along with them, accrue to people who did nothing to earn them.[2] Furthermore, if you divide all families into five groups according to their level of income, the Brookings Institution found that a child born to parents in the lowest income group is about eleven times more likely to remain in the same lowest income group than move to the highest income group (43 percent versus 4 percent). On the other hand, a child born into the highest income group is five times more likely to remain in that highest group than move to the lowest (40 percent versus 8 percent).[3] Unless children born into rich families emerge from the womb inherently smarter and more diligent, this is powerful evidence that our nation is not providing equal opportunity to all children.

Furthermore, the race of the family into which a child is born can also lead to significant inequities. Slavery may have ended in the 1860s and legal segregation may have ended in the 1960s, but they still exert a toll today. Prejudices don't change simply because a legislature changed some laws. Discrimination may not even significantly decline much after a change in the law because proving the law was violated is often very difficult. Additionally, the role bias plays may be subtle, but it can have a particularly marginalizing effect on victims precisely because it is so hard to identify and address.

The legacy of generations of inequality is readily apparent today. Communities remain highly segregated and life outcomes—from longevity to income—differ significantly by race. While there's been progress in the last few decades, one statistic shows how much further we have to go: In 2019, the median net wealth of a Black family was $24,100, while the median net wealth of a White family was $188,200.[4]

As difficult as it was to enact civil rights laws and end legal discrimination, actually living up to the ideals embodied in those laws will be more difficult. Investments in education and low-income neighborhoods are an essential part of this process. A more difficult part of this process is getting Americans to realize that promoting fairness and reducing inequality strengthens faith in the economic system, enables more people to be more productive, grows the pie, and thereby benefits everyone.

The impression that we are not all in this together is growing, dividing society and posing an increasing threat to our nation's stability and well-being. The situation is aggravated by how the concentration of resources at the top has enabled the wealthy to further insulate themselves in affluent enclaves with all sorts of private services. Their greater resources also allow even greater influence over the political system, affording those at the top even more advantages, making a bad situation worse.

I think every reader of this book is already well aware of our nation's growing economic divide, which has only accelerated since the onset of the coronavirus pandemic. There is no shortage of statistics showing how income gains for the top 1 percent have soared, how CEO salaries as a multiple of average worker salaries is at a record high, and how incomes for average workers have barely outpaced the cost of living. Although these trends are obvious, their causes may not be. So, that's what we'll discuss next.

WHY IS OUR ECONOMIC SYSTEM CREATING GREATER INEQUALITY?

The Winner-Take-All Economy

Let's go back just over a hundred years and think about the incomes of singers and musicians. Records, cassette tapes, compact discs, iTunes, and YouTube didn't exist. Instead, people heard music at live performances in theaters or music halls. If you wanted to hear music, that was your only option. As a result, many people in almost every city were able to earn a living as a singer or a musician. After all, you couldn't have the same musician playing at multiple locations at the same time. Some performers were better than others, and presumably they earned somewhat better livings. But there were a great many people employed this way, along with stagehands, ushers, ticket vendors, and so on, enabling them to support themselves and possibly a whole family on their earnings.

What has happened since then? The market for these performers and the jobs related to their performances has severely shrunk.

A handful of star performers dominate the international music business. Meanwhile, the music halls are gone and so are the local jobs that went with them. The amount of money spent on entertainment has not declined over the years. What has happened is that the spending is increasingly going to a few star performers.

The same holds true for furniture makers. Go to any museum with a collection of early American furniture and you'll see items made in most major cities. This is because most furniture was made locally. How much of your own furniture was made locally? Probably not much, if any. A few giant furniture makers, which are particularly attuned to consumer tastes and particularly efficient at production and distribution (like IKEA), dominate the industry. The local furniture makers are pretty much gone, and the earnings are now going to a much smaller number of huge furniture producers.

There's a pattern here. Yes, capitalism has always benefitted the most popular producers. The most well-liked performers received the highest incomes and the best furniture sold for the highest prices. And capitalism does create a powerful incentive for everyone to produce products and services that consumers want.

But something has changed since the days when there was room for many performers, many furniture makers, and many, many other producers. Incomes are increasingly concentrated among fewer and fewer super producers. This phenomenon is called the "winner-take-all" economy and rightly so. Today, the trend that eroded the roles for local performers and furniture makers is accelerating, limiting opportunities in more and more areas. Two of the most obvious current examples are the threat Amazon poses to the entire retail industry and the threat Google poses to the entire information industry. So, why is this happening?

The answer is the Technological Revolution (which, as we discussed, is part of the continued march of the Industrial Revolution). Recording technology has allowed a few great entertainers to perform on a global scale, rather than on the scale of one particular venue. Even more powerfully, it has allowed them to perform an infinite number of times based on just one recording. Technology, particularly the internet, has allowed retailers to sell their goods everywhere without having to negotiate for space in an unfamiliar city (or country), hire local employees, monitor the business via costly long-distance phone calls, or figure out the local rules and regulations. In essence, modern technology has greatly reduced, if not eliminated, the cost of doing business on a mass scale. This gives significant cost advantages (what businesspeople call "economies of scale") to the biggest providers and makes it very difficult for anyone else to compete with them.

Doing business on a mass geographic scale before advanced technology was always difficult and expensive. In the case of performers and many other service providers, it was literally impossible. That is no longer the case. Many areas of the economy can now be monopolized and exploited by a few large, talented providers using technology and the cost-free platform of the internet. In essence, the economy always produced winners who got to take more than others; now it produces winners who get to "take all."

This phenomenon affects all workers. When people have a variety of places to work as well as the option of starting their own business, they have more bargaining power when it comes to their wages and the other terms of their employment. They're also more likely to unionize. When the economy is dominated by a few gigantic organizations that can easily crush any start-up that might compete with them, workers are less likely to have leverage. The migration to online work during the coronavirus pandemic further reduced worker leverage as the pool of applicants for many jobs went from those in the local community to anyone on the planet with a high-speed internet connection.[5]

Making matters worse, the executives who run these behemoth businesses are fully aware of the greater control they have over workers and the regulatory system. Walmart's and Amazon's market power didn't just happen, and their success in preventing their employees from unionizing is not a coincidence. They worked long and hard to establish their clout in an environment where the stakes are higher than ever. The compensation, prestige, and, in fact, continued employment of these executives is dependent upon their keeping profits as high as possible. In the competition between each executive's own personal interest in their business's bottom line and the large number of workers whom they may not know, may never meet, and may be in a different city or nation, the bottom line is the clear favorite.

Automation and Artificial Intelligence

For those of us who have not hit home runs in this economy (or increasingly, not had parents or grandparents who hit home runs), advances in automation and artificial intelligence are becoming more and more of a threat to our economic well-being. What will happen if these trends continue and more jobs are lost to automation and artificial intelligence? How will displaced workers support themselves? Who will spend, and prevent the economy from shrinking?

"The future of work" is a hot topic and has pundits pontificating and many workers concerned that their jobs may be the next to be eliminated. Lawrence Katz, a labor economist at Harvard, estimates that 5 million Americans (almost 3 percent of the entire workforce) make their living driving taxis, buses, vans, trucks, and e-hailing vehicles. *All* of their jobs could be threatened by self-driving cars. Similarly, even though manufacturing *output* in the United States hit an all-time high in 2021[6] (yes, you read that correctly), the number of *jobs* in manufacturing is declining due to automation.

Is this something to be concerned about? I can ask the question a different way. Assume that each week you work forty hours and earn $1,500. Now, suppose you could use automation and artificial intelligence to enable you to reduce your weekly hours down to thirty while increasing your productivity so much that your earnings actually rise to $1,800. Would being offered that option (which you are free to reject) be a concern or problem for you? Clearly not. But that's the precise option automation and artificial intelligence offer to our society as a whole. Automation and artificial intelligence have the potential to greatly increase our economy's productivity—to increase the amount of output we as a nation can enjoy and simultaneously reduce the amount of work we as a nation have to do to produce it.

More stuff for less effort sounds great. When one person is offered that as a package deal, it's without doubt great because that person gets both benefits—more stuff and fewer work hours. But when that deal is offered on the aggregate societal level, it raises issues of who gets the extra stuff and whose work gets reduced. The people who get more stuff are not the same people whose jobs are downsized or eliminated altogether.

Automation and artificial intelligence, therefore, intensify the winner-take-all trend. The people who can compete on a global scale by employing (or creating) automation and artificial intelligence reap huge benefits. Meanwhile, the number of jobs and, therefore, the income and bargaining power of everyone else in the economy is diminished. These are powerful forces increasing income inequality, stoking resentment, and undermining faith in the system even more.

Accelerating inequality, however, is not inevitable. Many other advanced nations, particularly the Scandinavian nations and several nations in Eastern Europe, have managed to avoid the rapid rise in inequality that America has experienced.[7] These countries have similar economic systems to ours, so "capitalism" isn't to blame. In fact, there is no evidence that our economic system, which has brought so much prosperity to so many people over the last couple of centuries, is fundamentally flawed or that an alternative system would work better. There is, however, a lot of evidence that we have been remiss in regulating it and making sure our economy continues to provide opportunity for all.

Remember, the economy is like a highway: It needs rules to function properly. If we stand by and ignore problems that develop, like cars whizzing by at greater and greater speeds, crashes are inevitable. But before we can assess what we collectively need to do to reverse these troubling trends and enable the economy to function more effectively, we need to discuss much more about how the economy operates. After all, if you want to help fix a system, you need to understand it first. We start in the next chapter by discussing the most fundamental part of the economic system: money.

MONEY

What Do Gold, Dollars, and Cryptocurrencies Have in Common?

Money is the root of all evil.

—King James Bible

The lack of money is the root of all evil.

—Mark Twain

WHAT IS MONEY?

Money is probably the most important invention in the history of mankind. Almost every runner-up for "most important invention in the history of mankind" couldn't exist without money.

When the only goods were stone tools and animal hides, simply exchanging them for each other ("bartering") worked just fine. Bartering would not have worked just fine for the scientists who needed labs, microscopes, electricity, chemicals, syringes, and so on to develop the first antibiotics. They would have had to figure out just what to offer each of the thousands of suppliers of materials, goods, and services upon which their discovery depended. What could they offer the electric company to keep the lights on? The manufacturers to provide the necessary equipment? The glass company to provide the devices they needed? The assistant with the new baby at home to spend long hours at the lab? For that matter, if we were still using barter, would my supermarket, landlord, cable company, and so on be willing to take copies of this book in exchange for what they provide me? Money gave the answer to all of these countless questions and made antibiotics, this book, and almost every other good and service we take for granted possible.

Clearly, money has an enormous influence on us and our life choices. But before we can begin to assess its impact, we need to understand exactly what it is. While it's easy to give examples of money—for instance, the green slips of paper in your wallet—it can be a lot harder to define. That is where economists come to the rescue. They define "money" as anything that can be widely used to get all sorts of goods and services, what they call "a medium of exchange." Anything you can use to buy a sandwich at a local shop, a shirt on the internet, a cab ride on a city street, a ticket to a performance, or a house that is on the market is, by definition, "money." But to be useful, money also needs to meet two other tests. It must serve as a relatively stable store of value by more or less holding its value over time. (Fruit would not be useful as money since it rots.) It must also be easy to count. (Helium gas fails that test badly.)

Anything that meets these three tests—that serves as a medium of exchange, acts as a store of value, and is easy to count—is generally viewed as money. Historically, precious metals served this role (and are discussed more in the next section). In some prisoner of war camps, cigarettes served as money. Salt was once much more valuable than it is today and served as money as well. In fact, *salarium*, the Latin word for soldiers' payment in salt, serves as the basis for our word "salary."

In the modern economy, however, there is general agreement on what meets these three tests for money. Specifically, it's the currency in circulation (those green "notes" issued by the United States Federal Reserve, more commonly called the "Fed") and checking account balances at banks (which can be easily accessed by checks, debit cards, and phone apps).* Both can be immediately used to buy virtually anything for sale. Not much else has such universal acceptance, and, therefore, not much else is generally viewed as "money." If you're not sure of this, just go to a local shop or an internet seller and try to pay with gold, a stock certificate, Bitcoin, or almost anything other than "money" and see how far you get.

You may be thinking: What about credit cards? A lot of stuff is bought with credit cards. Credit cards, however, are not considered money because they simply allow you to delay payment for what you bought (hence, the term "credit") and pay later, presumably with "money" from your checking account.

You may be surprised to learn that currency not in circulation, meaning currency that's sitting in bank vaults or rolling off the government's printing presses, also doesn't count as money. Only currency in the hands of someone who can actually spend it, like a consumer, a business, the government, or a thief who stole currency from the bank and managed to get away, counts as money. So, although currency in bank vaults may look very much like money, it cannot be spent by anyone and, therefore, isn't money. (It does, however, have a role in our economy, which you'll hear all about when we discuss the Federal Reserve System and banking in chapter 11.)

There's another reason currency in bank vaults doesn't count as money. When someone deposits a twenty-dollar bill into their

---

* Money (currency and checking account balances) is also called "M1" or "the money supply." (Technically, it also includes the few dollars in traveler's checks.) There are other broader definitions of money, such as M2, which includes everything in M1 plus savings account deposits. Nevertheless, M1 is the widely accepted definition and is generally what people in finance, business, and economics mean when they talk about money.

checking account, they get a credit to their account in the exact same amount. To count both the $20 of currency now in the bank's vault (which cannot be spent) and the $20 increase in their checking account balance (which can definitely be spent) would overstate the amount of money in the economy. One form of money (the paper form) has merely been exchanged for or converted into another form of money (the electronic form).

The key point here is that the two forms of money (physical Federal Reserve notes in circulation and electronic credits in a checking account) are interchangeable. Your bank will be happy to convert one to the other. And if your bank doesn't have enough currency on hand, the Fed will be happy to ship them some. (You can tour the government's massive printing presses, which are capable of printing as much currency as needed.)† All that's happening when someone fills their wallet by making a withdrawal or feeds their checking account by making a deposit is that one form of money is being exchanged for another form of money. The total amount of money does not change when someone makes a withdrawal from or deposit to their account. At least not yet in this story.

Finally, when I taught economics, I always asked the class how much "money" Bill Gates had. The point of the question was not to marvel over his wealth (which is approximately $130 billion, as of this writing), but to emphasize that money is something different from wealth. Most of Gates's wealth is in corporate stock (particularly, Microsoft stock) and I bet very little of it is in money—currency and checking account balances. Money definitely counts as wealth, but the vast majority of people's wealth (especially wealthy people's) is not in money; it's in stocks, bonds, and real estate.

You may be thinking: Why are we bothering to precisely define money when we all know what it is? Because how money is

---

† The task of printing currency is delegated to the U.S. Treasury Department's Bureau of Engraving and Printing, not the Fed.

created, who creates it, and who gets it (and in what amounts) helps drive the economy. It's not some abstract idea, but rather something that has a direct and significant impact on everything from economic inequality to the economic cycle to what you and I choose to do for a living and how we live our lives. Understanding what money is and how it functions is critical to understanding the economy. Given its importance, the following section provides background on how money has developed over thousands of years and helps explain where we are today.

THE HISTORY OF MONEY

Commodity Money—the Original Money

There are four parts to this story. The first part is the simplest. The earliest money included gold, silver, shells, salt, and almost anything that was scarce and considered valuable. In particular, precious metals were commonly used as money, but not without all sorts of problems.

First, people had no easy way to assess the purity of the precious metals. Gold and silver coins could be debased. A coin that had 50 percent gold could be melted down to create two coins with 25 percent gold in each, and few people could tell the difference. Additionally, a large purchase required a good amount of physical strength, both to carry around all of the metal and to protect it from thieves (at a time when you couldn't just call 911). A small purchase might require the intervention of a specialized worker to divide up the piece of metal. Finally, the discovery of a new source of precious metal could make the discoverer very rich, but reduce the value of other people's holdings as the "precious" metal became somewhat less precious. Despite having problems with two of the three tests for money—issues of purity made it difficult to count and issues of scarcity made its value fluctuate—precious metals, and other scarce commodities, served as mediums of exchange and were considered to be money for thousands of years. But, as we discussed, technology has the potential to change everything.

Commodity-Backed Money—New and Somewhat Improved Money

The advent of the printing press in the fifteenth century enabled a new kind of money to become common in Europe—printed notes ("currency") that had a specific value clearly marked on their face and were usually issued by private bankers, like the Medicis of Florence, Italy. These notes were "backed" by precious metal sitting in the note issuer's vault. The issuers of the notes claimed that they had an amount of gold or silver equal in value to the notes they issued. Each note was similar to a receipt for an amount of precious metal equal to the face value of the note. If you wanted to redeem your note for real gold or silver, these issuers would be willing to provide it to you. But why would you bother? The paper notes were so much easier to carry, their value was so clearly noted, they were so readily available in various denominations, and, most importantly, they were so widely accepted by sellers of all sorts of goods and services.

The fact that these notes took on a life of their own created a problem. The private bankers who issued the notes were expected to have vaults full of precious metals to back them. But if they issued a few extra notes to lend to others who would repay the loans with interest that the bankers would pocket or issued a few extra notes for some other purpose, who would know? People rarely redeemed their notes for precious metal. As long as the bankers had enough gold or silver to meet the demand of the few oddballs who wanted to exchange their paper money for precious metals, they were set. The total "value" of all of the notes they issued could exceed the total value of the precious metals they were holding and no one would be the wiser.

Well, the bankers were set, until some of them got greedy. Once people caught on that some bankers might not have as much precious metal as their outstanding notes suggested they had, redemption requests surged, leading to a run on the bank. If the bankers did indeed issue too many notes and did not have enough precious metal to satisfy what was often a huge and unruly mob of people demanding to redeem their notes, the bank failed. If one bank failed, people became skeptical about the other banks, and then they too became inundated with redemption requests. These "bank run" crises occurred regularly and often ended violently, with dire consequences for the entire economy. This is one of the main reasons governments started taking over the business of issuing currency.

"Commodity-backed currency," the general name for this type of money, had a several-hundred-year run and was common until well into the twentieth century. It's the reason the British currency is called the pound sterling and the top of U.S. dollar bills often said "Silver Certificate" rather than "Federal Reserve Note" until 1964. The system may have worked better under government control than when private bankers were issuing currency, but it still had huge problems.

On one hand, the "gold standard," as it came to be known, prevented nations from issuing currency if they didn't have enough gold or other precious metal to back it. It made sure that governments didn't print too much currency and cause the existing currency to lose value. On the other hand, the gold standard was an economic straitjacket. It tethered the value of a nation's money to a relatively useless and rare metal over which the nation had no control. If a war broke out or a major economic downturn hit, creating the currency needed to address those crises was not an option. If a new discovery of gold in some far-off land reduced the metal's value, the nation's money would also lose value, putting the economy at risk.

This may all sound like obscure history, but almost every child unwittingly learns about the oppressive nature of the gold standard through L. Frank Baum's famous allegory *The Wizard of Oz*. The yellow brick road that's supposed to lead Dorothy and her friends to the solution for their problems? That's the gold standard. The land of Oz they are seeking? That's the abbreviation "oz," as in ounce of gold. The group follows the yellow brick road despite all sorts of perils along the way, only to find a useless old man from Omaha rather than any actual help. They would have all had an easier time achieving their goals had they just abandoned the road. The lesson that Dorothy and her friends learned was the same lesson that the governments of the world learned in the mid-twentieth century.

Fiat Money—Money from Nothing

In the 1930s, the Great Depression and the threat to civilization posed by World War II put a lot of pressure on governments. They faced a choice: They could choose to stick to the gold standard, not have enough money to respond to crises, and risk collapse. Or, they could abandon the gold standard and just create the money they needed. I'm sure you guessed it—they chose the latter.

So, what did that mean? Starting in 1931 in Britain and in 1933 in the United States (which is very recent if you look at the entire history of money), these governments began to dismantle the gold standard.‡ They started creating money not backed by anything, other than by a government decree that the money they created had value. This is called "fiat money." Governments say a twenty-dollar bill that they create has twenty times the value of a one-dollar bill that they create simply because they printed a "twenty" on one and a "one" on the other. There's literally nothing more to it than that. Currency today would be worth no more than the paper it's printed on, if not for everyone's agreement that it's worth more. How much more? Whatever amount the government printed on it.

Printing currency is simple. How the government gets that currency into the hands of someone who could actually spend it (in

‡ The United States completely abandoned the gold standard in 1971.

other words, into "circulation") and, thereby, convert it from a highly protected pile of paper imprinted with a lot of official writing to "money" as we have defined it, is not so simple. Chapter 11, which discusses the Federal Reserve System and how it controls the amount of money in circulation, will detail that convoluted process.

In the meantime, there's an important lesson to draw from fiat money: If money itself is probably the most important *invention* in the history of mankind, the universal agreement that money created out of thin air by the government has value is probably the most important *opinion* in the history of mankind. There is literally nothing else that every human on this planet agrees upon, whether it be the shape of the earth, the color of the sky, or the location of the Empire State Building. On the other hand, fiat money, the kind that fills our wallets and checking accounts, is objectively nothing more than something made up by the government. Yet, it has enormous value simply because everyone (literally, everyone) acts as if it has value and, in the case of currency, acts as if its value is equal to the number the government printer put on it. Obviously, this is great since, as we discussed, barter would no longer work in an economy with countless goods and services. But it's also great for another reason: It shows that we can all agree on something if it makes life easier and better, which fiat currency certainly does. That's a lesson that needs to be applied more widely.

Alternative Currencies—Future Money?

In the last few years, the government's monopoly on money has begun to look less certain. Will some alternative currencies start to compete with the dollar by becoming widely accepted as a medium of exchange and stable store of value? Is a new form of money emerging?

Before considering where we are headed, we have to strip away all of the hype and focus on precisely what alternative currencies are. They all have two distinguishing features: They are virtual currencies, meaning that they exist only electronically (not physically, like printed currency or metal coins), and, most importantly, they are issued by someone other than the government.

The obvious first question is: Who is issuing these alternative currencies? In most cases, it's not possible to tell, since the issuer can be literally anyone with some tech savvy or several hundred dollars to pay to one of the many web services that will help them set up a currency. The issuer may even be a *New York Times* journalist, such as David Segal who created his own cryptocurrency (which provided him with journalistic dividends, if not financial ones).[1] The murkiness of who is responsible for most of these alternative currencies is true even for Bitcoin, the largest alternative currency by far, whose founder is still not fully clear.[2]

Nevertheless, cryptocurrencies, like Bitcoin, have emerged as the leading alternative currencies. Cryptocurrencies are named after the sophisticated encryption algorithms they employ to make them secure and hard to counterfeit. As of this writing, there are a total of over $2.22 trillion worth of cryptocurrencies in circulation, up from zero in 2009.[3] Remarkably, the total value of cryptocurrencies is essentially the same as the total value of *all* U.S. currency in circulation (approximately $2.21 trillion).[4]

Almost every discussion of cryptocurrencies includes the blockchain technology on which they are based, their encryption techniques, the virtual "wallets" in which people hold them, the widely distributed electronic ledger of every transaction, the complicated methods for bringing new units of the currency into being (called "mining"), and the extraordinary amount of electricity the whole process consumes. If this were a book about technology or a book for someone looking to invest in cryptocurrencies (of which there is no shortage), those details would be relevant. Since this is a book about the economy, understanding those details is just as relevant to our discussion as understanding how the printer gets the ink on a twenty-dollar bill. As with so many concepts in business and economics, all sorts of irrelevant technical details get in the way of true understanding.

So, what is important about alternative currencies for our purposes? The vast majority of them have nothing backing them and have no intrinsic value. They are just like the fiat currencies we discussed in the last section, except that they are issued by someone other than the government. They are just digits in cyberspace. So, why do they have any value?

We know the U.S. dollar has value because it's always accepted as a medium of exchange. You not only *can* use the dollar, but also, with rare exceptions, you *must* use it to purchase things for sale and pay for obligations, including your taxes. Even a recent Bitcoin conference in New York City required payment in dollars for the attendance fee.

Meanwhile, each alternative currency has a certain value for the same reason a bar of gold, a Mickey Mantle baseball card, or the certified original electronic copy of a work of art (also called a non-fungible token or NFT) has a certain value: because the supply is limited and that is what other people are willing to pay for it. That's really all there is to it.

I think that's easy to understand intellectually, but most people have a hard time overcoming their gut sense that there must be something more to it—that there must be some underlying objective value. I remember visiting the Getty Museum in Los Angeles with my father and seeing the painting *Irises* by Vincent van Gogh. In 1987, a few years before the Getty acquired it, it became the most expensive painting ever sold, when a private investor bought it for approximately $54 million. My father said it was a bad, "cartoonish" painting and that 54 *dollars* would be too high a price for it.

I thought I could prove to him that an asset is worth a certain dollar amount not because of any objective reason (like its aesthetic quality) but simply because that is what other people were willing to pay for it. So, I asked him if a twenty-dollar bill had twenty times the aesthetic quality of a one-dollar bill. He thought

for a moment and then said, "Yes, it does to me." The only thing
this exchange wound up proving is the strong need many people
have to contrive some objective basis for the value of an asset,
even when clearly none exists.

We are still left with the question of why people are willing to
pay truly extraordinary amounts for some alternative currencies
and nothing for others (actually most others, if you look at the
great number of alternative currencies that have been launched
but have gone nowhere). The answer to that question would be
a great subject for a book on marketing, since little difference
objectively exists between most of these currencies. Maybe a person with a significant social-media presence owns a great amount
of a particular currency and promotes it to become rich(er).
Maybe people enjoy the online community that has developed
around some of these currencies. Maybe they like the image the
currency uses, such as the cute Japanese Shiba Inu dog of Doge-
coin, which started in 2013 as a joke and has reached a total valuation of approximately $32 billion. The fact that some currencies
flourish while almost-identical currencies fail is a reminder of one
of the core points of this book: Economics attempts to understand
human values and behavior, which, notwithstanding the claims of
some, cannot always be reduced to the kind of objective formulas
common in the hard sciences, like chemistry and physics.

So, will these currencies all crash and burn or will some survive
to become alternatives to the major currencies issued by national
governments? There is absolutely no way to know for sure, but
there are a few facts that might help us reach an informed opinion.

The first is that the issuers of alternative currencies are not
regulated like the Fed (which controls the U.S. dollar) or the central banks that issue the currencies of other nations, nor are their
activities anywhere nearly as transparent. The Fed's leaders and
the rules they are legally obligated to follow can be determined
with certainty—try figuring that out for Bitcoin or for most alternative currencies and you'll see what I mean by a lack of transparency. One of the consequences of this lack of regulation is that the

issuers of these alternative currencies (whoever they may be) may get greedy and start issuing more units of their currency, diluting the value of existing units. They almost all claim they will not or cannot do this, but how would someone using the currency go about enforcing that promise, or get compensated if the issuer fails to keep it?

This is true even of so-called stable coins, a type of cryptocurrency whose value is tied to an underlying asset that has a stable value, like the U.S. dollar. The idea is that the issuer of a stable coin holds the actual asset to which the coin is linked (the way governments used to hold gold to back their currencies). Therefore, the stable coin is supposed to be just a digital representation of a real asset and, thereby, have the same stable and objective value as the real asset.

Remembering the problems with the commodity-backed monies issued by the early private bankers will help you understand why "stable coins" may not be as stable as their name suggests. Try confirming who is holding what where and in what amount in connection with these currencies and their flaws will become immediately apparent. Even Tether, which is the largest stable coin and is linked to the dollar so that each "Tether token" has a value of $1, has failed to prove that it holds a number of dollars equal to the value of its outstanding currency. Furthermore, stable coins don't guarantee that they can be redeemed or exchanged for the real assets to which they are linked and that their issuers are supposedly holding.

A second important consideration regarding alternative currencies is that there may be flaws in the technology, making these currencies vulnerable to hacking, counterfeiting, or a whole host of other scams. To understand the magnitude of this problem, think about how difficult and frustrating addressing an issue with your bank account can be when you call customer service. Now think about how difficult and frustrating addressing that issue would be if your "bank" were some unregulated entity that only existed in cyberspace, was not affiliated with any real-live human beings, and did not even offer any customer service in the first place.

A third consideration is that the government may crack down on alternative currencies, viewing their issuance as a Ponzi scheme or a violation of the securities laws that govern selling "investments" to the public. The United States could ban alternative currencies entirely or, like China, make them more difficult to use by limiting the payment, storage, and other services that may be needed in connection with them. Such prohibitions may be hard to enforce, but they have the potential to tank values.

The government could also make trading in such currencies less alluring if it came up with a way to cut through the anonymity of the alternative currency marketplace. This would seriously impair one of the more significant current uses for alternative currencies—to pay for many illegal transactions, such as satisfying ransom demands by computer hackers. It would also enable governments to collect more of the tax that is legally due on any profits traders make, much of which, as of this writing, goes unreported to the tax authorities.

Another risk to alternative currencies is the potential for central banks to issue their own digital currencies (called central bank digital currency or CBDC). The central banks of a few Caribbean nations have already started to issue digital versions of their nation's currency, and many others, including the Fed, are looking into doing this. CBDCs have the transparency, credibility, and security that comes with official government issuance. On the other hand, CBDCs may raise privacy concerns for potential users, particularly those who use alternative currencies for illegal transactions. The key point is that if central banks embrace innovative technology and proceed with a digital version of money, alternative currencies could face a major competitive threat.

The likelihood of the government getting into the digital currency business or legally prohibiting or restricting alternative currencies is certain to increase if any of these currencies start to pose a threat to the government's monopoly on money. This monopoly enables the government to influence the economy through monetary policy (something you'll hear all about in part 4 of this book) and, therefore, the government is unlikely to give it up without a fight.

As of this writing, alternative currencies have a long way to go before they are widely accepted as money. Nevertheless, alternative currencies may continue to grow in value and importance, especially if they become easier to use and large organizations with some credibility start to issue them. For example, Facebook was, until recently, working on rolling out a virtual currency, Diem.

Historically, when people faced uncertainty and questioned the stability of their government, they bought gold or other tangible assets like diamonds. Cryptocurrencies now seem to be filling that role, at least to some extent. People are willing to attach multibillion-dollar valuations to currency units that are completely made up—fabricated out of thin air—by people who may not be known, who impose rules that may not be clear, and who use technology that we almost certainly do not understand. The future of cryptocurrencies may be uncertain, but their popularity speaks volumes about the lack of confidence people have in their governments and their traditional currencies.

INFLATION

Whatever type of money we are using or may be using in the future, inflation is always a possibility. Inflation is often defined as an increase in average prices, but can also be viewed as a decrease in the purchasing power of money. In other words, you could just as easily view a 5 percent increase in prices as a 5 percent decrease in the value of your money.

For now, we'll focus on a simple example to show how inflation can occur. Imagine an auction where a fixed number of play "dollars" are divided among the participants so that they can buy the goods on display. If the total number of play dollars were increased (remember, these play dollars have no value outside of this auction) without an increase in the number of goods for sale, people would be willing to bid and will, in fact, bid more and pay more for each good. Therefore, the bids, or prices, for each of these goods will go up—there will be inflation. For example, if the number of play dollars were increased by 10 percent, you would expect people to bid 10 percent more on average for each good—there will be inflation of 10 percent. You can also look at inflation as shrinking the value of each existing dollar by 10 percent, since each dollar will get you 10 percent less stuff after the total number of dollars is increased.

Our economy usually works the same way, but on a much larger scale. If the nation's supply of money grows faster than the total supply of goods and services, prices will, on average, increase. Inflation, as economists like to say, is essentially too much money chasing too few goods.

Another way to picture this important relationship is to imagine the huge pool of money that is America's total money supply—currency plus checking account balances. Just as in the auction example, the price of all goods and services is determined by the size of the pool of money relative to the size of the pool of goods and services. If the pool of money grows faster than the pool of goods and services, there is inflation. If it grows slower, there is deflation (or, negative inflation). If it is growing at the same rate, prices are stable.

Inflation, like many things, is relatively harmless in moderation, although it can be disastrous otherwise. This disaster scenario is called "hyperinflation," which means accelerating and out-of-control price increases that ultimately render money worthless. We'll discuss hyperinflation in chapter 11, when we detail how our government maintains control over the amount of dollars in circulation and how other governments in the past lost control over the amount of their nation's money.

Recently, inflation has ticked up primarily due to production difficulties caused by the coronavirus pandemic (often called "supply chain disruptions") and oil supply issues caused by war in Ukraine. Nevertheless, as of this writing, both of these problems, and the price increases they are causing, are expected to be mostly

temporary. In any event, notwithstanding the cries of some politicians trying to justify cuts in government spending, there is no
indication that hyperinflation and the out-of-control increase in the
money supply that would produce it are anywhere on the horizon.

THE FINANCIAL ECONOMY VERSUS THE REAL ECONOMY

Many people confuse the financial economy with the real economy. The financial economy is the pool of money: the green slips
of paper printed by the government and the electronic entries in
our bank accounts. As we know, there is absolutely no limit on
how much money can be created out of thin air. The amount of
money is simply a number controlled by the Fed. The only reason
money has value is because people are willing to exchange it for
real goods and services.

The real economy, on the other hand, is that pool of real goods
and services that are produced and consumed. These goods and
services are measured in dollars by the financial economy, but
they are much more than just numbers. They keep us fed, housed,
clothed, groomed, informed, and alive. They're the product of all of
our labors, which means that, unlike money, they can't be increased
by simply pushing a few buttons on a computer at the Fed.

Creating more money can definitely increase the price of stuff,
but it will not necessarily increase the amount of stuff. And the
amount of stuff is all that really matters for our well-being. Inflating prices is like inflating the scores on a test—the grades may go
up, but the students are no more knowledgeable.

I wrote that creating more money "can" increase prices rather
than "will" in the last paragraph for a reason. In the auction analogy, more money will definitely cause inflation. If the play money
is increased by a certain percent and the goods for sale stay the
same, there will be inflation equal to the percent increase in the
play money. In the real world, however, more money *can* (under

certain circumstances) actually cause more goods and services to be produced—the financial economy *can* impact the real economy. Imagine if giving the bidders more play dollars caused the number of goods at the auction to increase, or if inflating the scores on a test made students smarter.

How can this made-up world of green slips of paper and electronic entries in bank accounts affect the amount of stuff in the real economy? It is because, to a large extent, people confuse the two worlds and act in the real world based on changes in the financial world. When people see more money around, they begin to act as if the real economy is actually growing. Consumers start spending more and, if there is slack in the economy, businesses start hiring and producing more. This confusion between the financial world and the real world is what enables the government to help manage the economy and get us out of economic slumps. We will discuss how the government manages this confusion in chapter 12, when we discuss monetary policy.

In the meantime, whether or not changes in the amount of money affect how much total stuff America produces, it can also affect who gets what since some prices go up more than others. Inflation is an *average* increase in prices and includes the cost of *all* goods and services, including the cost of labor. Since labor costs are the most significant production cost, rising inflation should *on average* raise wages and salaries. As with any average, however, some wages will be above average and some will be below, sometimes far above and far below. If there is a wide variation, an average can be very misleading. Think about the fact that the "average" adult human being has one breast and one testicle.

Lately, the wages of many workers in the middle and low end of the pay scale have not been increasing as fast as those of workers at the high end (remember CEOs and Wall Street executives are "workers" and what they earn are "wages"). As we discussed, we have become more of a winner-take-all economy. There is much more on this growing divide in this book. But the point here is that inflation by itself, unlike the trends discussed in the last chapter, is not a significant contributor to this inequality. Inflation is just an average. Whether inflation is high, low, zero, or negative, some workers will have their wages go up more than the average and some will not.

The problem is not the average change in wages, but who gets more than the average and by how much and who gets less than the average and by how much. And that is determined by the trends in our economic system undermining opportunity and promoting inequality. These trends threaten to undermine the whole purpose of our economic system: to make our lives better and satisfy as many of our needs and wants as possible. Therefore, we look at how that system affects us as individuals in the next part of this book. We discuss the size of the economic pie, how it is divided up, and how it is affected by international trade.

Part II

PEOPLE

4

SPENDING, PRODUCTION, AND INCOME

How Big Is Our Economy, and Why Does It Matter?

People often say "Money makes the world go round" . . . but actually it's the world (global, economic, political, and social events) that makes the money go round.

—Savannah Jackson, financial advisor

ONE PERSON'S SPENDING IS ANOTHER PERSON'S INCOME

One of the most fundamental relationships in economics is the one between what people spend and what people earn. This relationship, like most economic relationships, can become clear to anyone thinking about the economy—formulas, charts, and complicated graphs aren't necessary. In particular, if you add up every American's annual income* it would equal total spending on goods

---

* The term "income" can mean different things in different contexts. In this context, income means the sum of all wages, profits from businesses, interest, and rents (with certain technical adjustments). In the tax context, income has a somewhat different meaning. For example, it does not include business profits

and services made in America in that year (assuming you adhere to certain accounting conventions).

Every economics textbook has an equation with several different variables to show this relationship in a formal way. In my opinion, this equation, like so many others that appear in books on economics, doesn't aid (and may actually diminish) most people's understanding. The key to understanding what's going on in the world is to focus on what's going on in the world.

Since the relationship between income and spending is so important, I'll give three examples, rather than an equation, to help explain it. First, if I buy a new book on Amazon for $20, I spent $20 and someone earned $20. That "someone" is actually a group of people, usually including a literary agent, an editor, the owners of the business that publishes the book, a marketing guru, the workers and shareholders of Amazon, and possibly even an author. The sum of all the income due to my purchase of the book is exactly $20.

Similarly, if a firm spends $20 million designing and implementing new software for their computers, a total of $20 million in incomes is earned by coders, existing employees who get overtime pay to learn the new system, and all of the other people involved in providing and setting up the new computer system.

Finally, if the government spends $5 billion for a wall on the southern border, a total of $5 billion in incomes is created for the workers who build the wall, the providers of building equipment, engineers, countless consultants to the government, and everyone else involved in providing some good or service in connection with it. The bottom line is that all income is due to spending on new goods and services by people, businesses, or the government.

Since incomes depend on spending, is a person's decision to save more and spend less a bad thing because it destroys income? We are almost always told by financial advisors, parents, friends,

---

if they stay within the business (in other words, they are not distributed to the business owners), but would include the gain made on the sale of an asset, such as a person's home. In other contexts, income can mean just the salary someone gets paid.

and even economists that saving some of our income rather than spending it all on stuff is a good thing. But the more one person saves, the less others earn. So, how can saving money be a good thing?

This issue is called the paradox of thrift, and it highlights that what is good for one person to do (save more) can cause harm (lower total incomes) if everyone does it. You can compare increasing your savings to moving over to the side of a small, crowded boat sailing into New York Harbor. It makes sense for you to move to the side of the boat that gives you a view of lower Manhattan. But, if everyone decides to do the same sensible thing that you're doing, the boat capsizes, and the view is the last thing you'll be thinking about as you swim to shore.

The same is true of the economy. Saving more does often make sense for each of us as individuals. Some minor sacrifices in spending can make our futures more secure and enable us to do things we otherwise wouldn't have been able to do. And in the real world, someone's decision to spend less and save more is often offset by someone's decision to spend more and save less. But if everyone starts to save more, incomes drop. And what happens when incomes drop? People spend even less. And what happens when people spend even less? Incomes drop even more. And what happens when incomes drop even more? I think you get the picture by now. The economy tanks.

THE GROSS DOMESTIC PRODUCT

In 2020, people spent approximately $20.9 trillion on new goods and services produced in the United States and, therefore, created $20.9 trillion of total income in the United States.[1] That number also happens to equal another number that you may already be familiar with: the nation's gross domestic product (GDP). GDP for a given year is defined as the dollar value (in other words, the sale price) of all goods and services produced in the nation in that year.

It includes what you paid for your shirt, your haircut, and this book (if anything); what the government paid for new roads and teachers' salaries; and what businesses paid for security services and new computer equipment. Think of the GDP as our economy's report card—it tells us how much we as a nation produced in a given year.

There are books devoted to explaining the detailed rules for calculating GDP, total spending, and total incomes. The most important of these rules are geared toward ensuring that this economic report card is accurate by confirming that the nation gets credit for all of the goods and services it produces in that year, but nothing else.

For example, GDP would not be credited with the resale of goods produced in a previous year, such as sales of used goods, which includes existing homes.[†] Those goods would be counted in the GDP of the year in which they were produced. Nor would GDP be credited with sales of goods that were produced by foreigners. Similarly, it would not be credited for "sales" that are mere transfers of assets, such as sales of stocks, bonds, precious metals, or land. Such sales just involve someone with a pile of cash and someone with the asset swapping positions—no goods or services are *produced* for someone's benefit, and therefore the nation should not be given any credit for it in its economic report card. Finally, the sale of inputs to businesses that are in turn used to produce other goods, like glass and steel for a car manufacturer, are not included. If they were, the GDP would be inflated. A car sold for $30,000 should add just $30,000 to GDP, not $30,000 plus what the car manufacturer paid for the steel and glass (and the labor and all sorts of other inputs). The key point for us is that with a few technical adjustments[‡], spending on new and final (in other words, ready to be put to use) goods and services equals GDP.

[†] If part of the price paid for a used good is a fee for a service in connection with the sale, that part of the price is included in GDP. For example, although the sale of an existing home would not be included in GDP, the fee the broker charged, as well as all of the other fees paid out of the sale price, would be included in GDP.

[‡] For example, goods produced in a given year, added to inventories, and actually sold in the next year are counted in the GDP of the first year.

It's not a coincidence that each year's GDP equals total spending on goods and services made in America that year, which equals total U.S. incomes for that year. It also makes sense that it's not a coincidence that if we spent $20.9 trillion on new goods or services, then we produced $20.9 trillion of new goods or services and $20.9 trillion was earned as a result. In the examples from the last section, the new book would have contributed $20 to GDP, the new computer system would have contributed $20 million to GDP, and the wall would have contributed $5 billion to GDP. Spending equals incomes equals GDP.

Finally, just as the GDP can tell us how much our economy produces at any point in time, it can also tell us how much it has improved over time. The only problem with comparing the GDP of one year with that of another year is that part of the change is due to price changes (inflation). So, if output from one year to the next year stayed exactly the same, but prices rose, the GDP would go up, but we would be no better off.

Therefore, to measure the *real* growth in the economy over time, economists subtract out price increases due to inflation—this is called "real GDP" growth since it measures the growth of actual output. On average, the U.S. economy, as measured by real GDP, has grown by just over 3 percent per year since the end of World War II. The earlier part of that period had higher growth than the more recent part. Since 2000, real GDP growth has slowed to an average of approximately 1.8 percent a year and some economists fear the growth rate will continue to slow (what they call "secular stagnation").[2]

IS MORE NECESSARILY BETTER?

Rankings are popular, and GDP figures allow people to rank national economies by the total value of goods and services they produce. As of this writing, the United States ranks number one in total GDP, although number-two China is often predicted to move into first place in the next few years. Many economists, national leaders, businesspeople, and international investors view these statistics as indications of how well people in each nation are doing. Are they right?

We have already discussed the first problem with using GDP as a measure of well-being: GDP simply equals the sum of the sale prices paid for each good and service. Since computers have dropped in price but soared in quality, each new computer contributes less to GDP, but makes people better off. Since families used to purchase encyclopedias to help educate their children and now all that information (and much, much more) is available online for free, encyclopedia sales contribute less to GDP, but people are better off. If I grow vegetables organically in my backyard rather than buy the stuff wrapped in multiple layers of plastic at the supermarket, the lost grocery sales reduce GDP, but I am (and the environment certainly is) better off. If crime declines and we spend less money on security systems and police protection, GDP is reduced, but we are clearly much better off. These examples show the limitations of using GDP as a precise indicator of people's true well-being.

The second problem arises when we try to compare the GDPs of different nations, each of which has a different currency. In order to do that, the GDP figures for each nation need to be converted to a common currency in order to be compared. The common currency most often used is the U.S. dollar, which raises the question of how to do that conversion. Simply using prevailing exchange rates can cause significant distortions.

Exchange rates are determined by currency traders who buy and sell each nation's currency, creating a global market for the currencies of most nations. In this market, people trade their local currency for another nation's currency when they wish to import something from or make an investment in the other nation. Therefore, the goods, services, and assets that are bought and sold on international markets, like oil, televisions, government bonds, and other "tradeable" goods, determine exchange rates. Those are the goods people acquire foreign currency to purchase and, therefore, they determine the value of the foreign currency. What a local person has to pay for goods and services that are only sold locally, like haircuts, housing, schooling, and fresh local food (what economists call "non-tradeable" goods), has little to no effect on exchange rates. What does this mean for us?

It means that the GDP of a nation with inexpensive non-tradeable, local goods would understate how well people are doing. You can guess which nations typically have inexpensive non-tradeable, local goods—poorer nations. They have cheap land, labor, and other inputs that make local goods relatively inexpensive compared to similar goods in wealthier nations. For example, housing is a particularly important non-tradeable good (it's fixed to the ground, cannot be exported, and, except for some very high-end properties, is almost exclusively bought locally). You can easily see how much more housing you could get in a poorer nation than you would get in the United States for the same amount of money converted into dollars. Identical housing in Mexico and the United States would therefore add less to Mexico's GDP since it would cost less. On the other end of the spectrum, the GDP of a nation with expensive non-tradeable goods, rich nations like Switzerland and Luxembourg, would overstate how well people are doing due to the inclusion of the high cost of such goods in their GDPs.

Economists have tried to account for these distortions by converting the GDP of each nation into dollars using "purchasing power parity" (PPP) exchange rates. To do this, they first determine the amount of local currency that would be needed to purchase a large bundle of consumer goods in each nation. The PPP exchange rate is the exchange rate that would enable someone to buy the same bundle of goods in the United States. The goal is that when the GDP of another nation is converted into dollars, it's converted at a rate that reflects the local currency's actual buying power in the local economy. In other words, PPP exchange rates try to compare the number of apples in one nation to the number of apples in another nation (the real economy) rather than the price of apples in one nation to the price of apples in another (the financial economy).

This all seems very scientific until you think about how difficult assembling the identical bundle of goods in each nation would be, especially given how widely the quality of local goods and services can vary. Furthermore, every nation has a significant informal economy based on cash transactions, and many have a significant black-market economy, both of which are unlikely to be fully captured in the data. Economists make estimates for these sectors and try to incorporate them into the GDP figures. Nevertheless, the poorer a nation, the larger these sectors of the economy typically are, and the more the GDP calculation for those nations may be understated.

Finally, for GDP figures to mean anything about the well-being of the average person, we need to know two facts. The first is how many people live in the nation so that GDP per person (or per capita, as it's more commonly called) can be calculated. When nations are ranked by GDP per capita, the United States still does very well. The United States is far ahead of China because China's economic output, which is similar to America's, has to be divided among more than four times as many people.

The second fact we need to know is how evenly the GDP is divided among the population. If a nation has significant income inequality, the typical person in that nation may be worse off than the typical person in a more egalitarian nation with a substantially lower GDP. How equitably incomes are distributed in a nation is difficult to calculate precisely. The most common measure of income inequality is the Gini index, which provides a score for income dispersion. A score of 0 means everyone in the nation earns the same amount, and a 100 means 100 percent of all income is earned by one person and everyone else earns nothing.[3] According to a report by the World Bank, the Gini indexes for "Communist" China and Vietnam (38.5 and 35.7, respectively) were *higher* (implying *more* income inequality) than "Capitalist"

Germany and Canada (31.9 and 33.3, respectively).[4] The United States, with an index of 41.4, has more income inequality than all four of those nations, as well as virtually every other major industrialized nation.

The Gini index has become increasingly important in assessing a typical person's economic well-being as economic inequality increases. For example, while Sweden has a slightly lower GDP per capita than the United States, the typical Swede is likely to be economically better off than the typical American due to a more equal distribution of incomes. (Sweden has a Gini index of 30.0.)

Even if we ignored all of these issues and the GDP allocable to a typical person in a nation can be definitively calculated, how important is more? The answer to this question, like the answer to almost every question in economics, can be determined by looking around and observing. Is someone with an annual income of $63,414 better off than one with $8,329? These are the 2020 GDP per capita amounts[5] for the United States and Mexico according to the World Bank. I think most people would agree that a difference of that magnitude is significant. But what about a smaller difference, such as the one between the United States and Germany ($46,208), Sweden ($52,274), or even the United Kingdom ($41,125) or Switzerland ($87,097)?

Differences in GDP per capita between the United States and other wealthy nations may be primarily due to the fewer hours most people work in those other nations when compared to the United States. Shorter workweeks, longer family care leaves, earlier retirements, and more vacation days reduce GDP, but do they really make people worse off? Therefore, these relatively small differences in GDP may mean literally nothing.

GDP's significant limitations in assessing well-being has spawned several measures that attempt to directly measure well-being using a variety of factors such as longevity, nutrition, personal freedom, safety, education, and health-care access. One is them is the Social Progress Index, which was inspired by the research of several prominent economists. The index collects fifty metrics of

well-being to produce "a comprehensive measure of real quality
of life, independent of economic indicators."[6] The United States
ranks twenty-fourth on this index. Other measures of well-being
have also ranked the United States significantly below where it
ranks in GDP per capita.

Nevertheless, a much higher GDP per capita does mean,
on average, access to more goods and services. Access to more
doesn't necessarily guarantee a better life, but it can enable it.
Just as a high-income family can squander its resources, a high
GDP nation can waste a lot of its production on pointless foreign
engagements, excessive security, a massive health-care bureaucracy, or costly incarceration to punish people who break the
law but pose no threat to society. On the other hand, just as a
low-income family can use its resources wisely, a low GDP nation
can spend its resources on education (making its citizens more
productive), infrastructure (making its economy more efficient),
and quality-of-life measures (reducing the economic loss that bad
health, crime, and other social ills cause).

An economy that produces more does, at the very least, provide
the opportunity for a better life. So, if life is not getting better as
GDP per capita increases, the problem is not with the amount of
production—it's with who is getting the spending power and what
they are doing with it. The next section addresses those questions.

WHO IS SPENDING?

Spending on goods and services in the United States comes from
four sources: (1) $14.1 trillion by American consumers (approxi-
mately 330 million people like you and me, on literally countless
goods and services); (2) $3.6 trillion by domestic businesses (on
buildings, machinery, equipment, software, patents, and all of the
other goods and services they use to produce stuff); (3) $3.9 tril-
lion by our government (federal, state, and local branches combined); and (4) $2.1 trillion by foreign consumers, businesses, and

governments (when they buy U.S.-produced goods and services that we export). The sum of all four categories of spending is $23.7 trillion, which exceeds our GDP by $2.8 trillion. Why is that? Part of what Americans spend money on is foreign-made goods and services (imports) and our GDP (our economic report card) should not be credited with things we bought but did not produce. Specifically, we spent $2.8 trillion on imports. If we deduct that from total spending, we get $20.9 trillion, which equals our GDP.[7] (There is much more to discuss about imports and exports, the subject of chapter 6.)

You may have noticed that the portion of our GDP spent by the U.S. government seems low. The budget of the federal government alone was $4.45 trillion in 2019 and rose to $6.55 trillion in 2020 primarily due to the coronavirus pandemic.[8] When the budgets of state and local governments are included, the total rises to $6.8 trillion in 2019 and $8.8 trillion in 2020.[9] So, how can total spending on goods and services by all levels of government equal only $3.9 trillion? Because more than half of the money in government budgets is not *spent* by the government on goods and services—it's simply *transferred* to individuals (through programs such as Social Security, student aid, and food stamps) or businesses (through programs such as grants and subsidies) for *them* to spend.

You can think of the government's budget as divided into two categories. We have already discussed the first category: money the government spends on goods and services. This includes spending on national defense, health care, roads, teachers, and police, to name just a few of the goods and services the government purchases each year.

The other, larger category is the money the government simply transfers to others to spend. For example, in 2020, the federal government's budget included approximately $1.1 trillion for Social Security, approximately $95 billion for the Supplemental Nutrition Assistance Program (more commonly called food stamps), and approximately $46 billion for subsidies to American farmers.[10] These programs are examples of "transfer payments," which means the government does not spend this money in the economy, but merely transfers it to people or businesses for them to spend in the economy. Transfer payments allow the government to reallocate money among Americans. The government takes spending power from some (by taxing them or borrowing from them) and reallocates it to others (by providing the transfer payment to them). Therefore, as we will discuss in the last part of this book, transfer payments can play an important role in addressing the problem of growing income inequality.

Economists call the United States economy a consumer economy because consumer spending is the majority of all spending and therefore the driver of what gets produced. What consumers directly spend actually understates the importance of consumers. Without spending by consumers, there would be little reason for businesses to spend on things like factories, tools, equipment, office buildings, and computers, which they need to produce all of the goods and services people buy.

This fact is often conveniently ignored by those who claim that lower taxes on the wealthy will grow the economy and create more jobs. This argument has gone by many names, including Reaganomics, trickle-down economics, and supply-side economics, and remains popular among a good number of people on the right side of the political spectrum. Their argument is that the wealthy are more likely to have mostly everything they want, so they are more likely to save any additional money they get from a tax cut than a non-wealthy person would. That much is true.

What is not true is that more savings will lead to more investment by businesses, a growing economy, and new jobs. That claim violates the most important rule for understanding the economy: Use common sense. What competent businessperson would invest to grow their business without additional demand for their product? On the other hand, if there really is demand for their product, they would find a way to finance expansion regardless of whatever tax rate wealthy people were paying. If there is no additional demand for their product, any offers to finance expansion would land on deaf ears.

Since businesses expand to meet greater demand for their products and services, a more effective way to grow the economy and create jobs would be to concentrate the tax cuts on lower-income people. Just as the wealthy are more likely to save the money they receive from a tax cut, the less well-off are more likely to spend the money they receive from a tax cut, creating demand for more goods and services. If tax cuts are focused on the wealthy, a bit may "trickle down" to other Americans. If tax cuts or other financial benefits, such as debt relief or cash-transfer payments, are focused on the non-wealthy, virtually all of it will be fairly quickly spent on new goods and services, causing businesses to invest and grow the economy to meet that new demand.

Clearly, who is spending and how much they are spending is determined by how much income and wealth they have. How that income is earned and that wealth is accumulated is the subject of the next chapter.

5

WORK INCOME, INVESTMENT INCOME, AND WEALTH

How Is Income Divided between Labor and Capital?

I made my money the old-fashioned way. I inherited it.

—John Raese, businessman and former chairman
of the West Virginia Republican Party

WHO IS EARNING?

As we discussed in the last chapter, every dollar of spending on American-produced goods and services creates a dollar of income for Americans.* So, how do the trillions of dollars of spending get to us as income? There are only two ways.

The first way is as wages, salaries, tips, bonuses, and other income due to work. This category includes everything from a

---

* Money someone receives as income can be transferred from them to another person for that other person to spend. Such transfers can be voluntary, such as inheritances and gifts, or involuntary, such as tax payments to fund government transfer programs. This section focuses on who gets the income originally and not to whom some of the money from that income may be transferred.

minimum-wage worker's hourly pay to a CEO's multimillion-dollar annual bonus. We'll call this category "work income." If you add all of it up, you can view it as the share of our GDP going to labor.

The second way income gets to us is as "investment income." This category includes profits from businesses, interest payments on money loaned to others, and rents from property rented out.[†] If you add up all investment income, you can view it as the share of our GDP going to the owners of capital (in other words, assets that produce income).

This latter category is even bigger than people think because every dollar of profit at a business is really a dollar of income for its owners. That's true even if that dollar is left in the business's bank account rather than distributed to its owners as a dividend or a return of capital. Businesses are not people. They may own assets and earn profits, but they are in turn owned by real human beings who are the ultimate owners and beneficiaries of those assets and profits. The profits left in the business after the business has paid all of its expenses, wages, taxes, and other obligations are no less the money of the owners of the business than if the money were distributed to them. Just because cash remains in the business account and isn't moved to the personal accounts of the owners doesn't change the fact that the cash belongs to the owners.

So, what has been happening to the division of our GDP between labor and capital? According to the McKinsey Global Institute, labor's share of all income in the United States dropped from 63.3 percent in 2000 to 56.7 percent in 2016 (meaning

---

† A business owner can have both work income and investment income from their business. The pay they receive for the work they do in the business would be work income and the profits they take would be investment income. In smaller businesses, the distinction between the two may be unclear—a shop owner may consider their income to be a profit on their investment in the shop, when really the shop only survives because of their work behind the counter. Nevertheless, the tax code has very detailed rules for distinguishing one from the other.

capital's share increased from 36.7 percent to 43.3 percent).[1] This shift in income from labor to capital is also highlighted by the fact that in the same sixteen-year period, our GDP increased 82 percent while median net compensation for workers increased only 46 percent.[2] Given our discussion in the last chapter, I'm sure many of you have already correctly concluded that if work income is growing slower than GDP, investment income is growing faster than GDP. In the last couple of decades, most major nations have also seen a declining share of income going to labor, although not by as much as the United States has.[3]

In essence, the typical worker is getting hit doubly hard. The share of the total economic pie going to labor has been decreasing while, as we discussed in chapter 2, that shrinking share is more and more unequally divided between those at the top and everyone else. So why is the share going to capital growing?

WEALTH BEGETS WEALTH

Just as all work income is due to labor, all investment income is due to wealth—the ownership of capital that produces the investment income. Wealth is composed primarily of stocks (which represent ownership of a business), bonds (which represent money owed to the bond's owner), physical assets (such as real estate that can be rented out), and bank account balances. As of this writing, there is approximately $145,000,000,000,000 (that is $145 trillion) of wealth in the United States.[4] The assets that comprise wealth are generally accumulated by people over time—sometimes over very long periods of time, as in the case of inherited wealth, which, as we discussed, accounts for more than half of all wealth in the United States.

Having wealth is arguably more beneficial than having income. Wealth is a store of value that can be accessed at any time for any purpose and is not dependent on continuing to show up for a job. Of particular importance to this discussion, wealth also almost always creates additional wealth by earning income for its owners and appreciating in value over time. Billionaire Edgar Bronfman Jr. once commented on this phenomenon by saying, "To turn $100 into $110 is work. To turn $100 million into $110 million is inevitable." In other words, lower-income people struggle to save money and face limited investment options due to the small size of their savings, whereas wealthy people have money left over after their spending, as well as access to the best investment opportunities the economy provides.

When investments grow in value, as the vast majority do over significant periods of time, that increase in value is not taxed at all until the owner actually sells the investment and pockets the gain. For example, even though Jeff Bezos's wealth increased by approximately $75 billion in 2020 due to the increase in value of his Amazon stock, he did not owe any tax on that gain and will not owe any tax on that gain until he sells it. On the other hand, the median salary for U.S. full-time Amazon employees was $37,930 in 2020,[5] and each of those employees was subject to tax on the entire amount.

When assets such as stock are finally sold, the tax code has a special lower tax rate, called the "capital gains tax rate," for the profits investors earn. The capital gains tax works as follows: When someone buys stock (or any asset for that matter) for $100,000 and they sell it, let's say, five years later for $160,000, there is a "capital gain" of $60,000. There will be a tax on that gain only at the end of the five-year period when the stock is sold, even though the stock could have been increasing in value each year during that period. Finally, that $60,000 gain will be subject to those lower capital gain tax rates. (The $100,000 of the $160,000 sale price is just a return of capital, which is understandably tax free since it's just a return of the person's original investment.)

What does this mean? Wage income, the money people earn from their work, is almost always taxed at higher rates than investment income, which is concentrated among wealthier taxpayers. Warren Buffett, who has a fortune estimated to be around $80 billion, famously called attention to how he pays a lower percentage of his income in taxes than his secretary. This is due to the lower tax rate for capital gains, which is how he earns his money, and the higher tax rate for wage income, which is how his secretary earns her money.

In addition to growing in value over time, many assets provide regular payments to their owners while they're owned. These include dividends[‡] on stocks, interest on bonds, and rents on real estate. Much of this income is also taxed at lower rates than income earned from work. Even if assets don't provide any income before they're sold (like a second home that the owner doesn't rent out or a stock that doesn't pay a dividend), owners receive benefits from the growth in value of their investment. These untaxed benefits include the ability to borrow money at lower interest rates using the growing value of their assets as collateral, the financial security that greater wealth provides, the ability to convert their gains to cash as needed, and, in the case of a second home, a place to spend some time.

One justification offered for not taxing people each year on the increase in value of their assets is that it's difficult to know how much the assets have gone up in value over the course of the year. That, however, is not true for publicly traded stocks and bonds, which constitute the majority of all wealth in America. The increase in the price of a share can be looked up and the gain over the course of the year can be easily determined.[§] Nevertheless, the gain is not taxed.

Another justification for not taxing the increase in the value of assets is that corporations pay taxes to the government on their profits and therefore the gain to the shareholder is reduced by the

---

[‡] Dividends are a distribution of profits by a company to its owners (in other words, its shareholders). The company can distribute them on a regular basis (such as quarterly) or whenever it sees fit.

[§] In the event of a loss due to a decrease in the price of a share, the shareholder could be given a credit against their gains. That is how it works with regard to gains and losses on shares that are sold; the same system could work for gains and losses on shares that are not sold.

amount of those taxes. The tax on corporate profits, as of this writing, is 21 percent. Due to the tax law's complexity and abundance of loopholes, the average rate paid by the five-hundred largest American corporations in 2018 was actually 11.3 percent, and ninety-one of the five-hundred largest companies paid nothing at all.[6] The companies that paid no taxes include Amazon, Chevron, Halliburton, and IBM, some of the most successful companies in the world.

The question remains: When income from investments is finally received by the investor, why does the United States almost always tax it at a significantly lower rate than income from work? The politicians who support this lower rate for investment income argue that it gives investors an incentive to invest. So, would investors simply stuff their savings into a mattress if they had to pay a larger percentage of their investment gains in taxes? If an investment will yield 6 percent profit and the tax on the profit goes up, do they decide that zero profit is preferable and choose not to invest?

On the other hand, doesn't a higher tax rate on earned income discourage work and productive participation in the economy? Maybe not for the prime earner for a family with children. But for older workers, workers marginally attached to the labor force, and some other groups, a change in take-home pay can make a difference in their decision to take a job or not. To see through the arguments of those who support lower tax rates for capital gains does not require training in economics. Like so much else, it just requires the application of common sense.

Clearly, wealth begets wealth and the more a person has, the more they can accumulate. These tax advantages for investment income combined with soaring income inequality and mounting inheritances are causing wealth to become even more concentrated. There are many estimates of just how concentrated wealth in America has become, from the Federal Reserve Bank of St. Louis's estimate that 77 percent of all wealth is held by the richest 10 percent of households[7] to the Congressional Budget Office's estimate that the bottom half of all families own just 1 percent of all wealth.[8] Unless something is done to make the playing field more level, this disparity is likely to result in a continually increasing concentration of wealth (and, therefore, power) in a relatively small group of people.

This phenomenon is the focus of Thomas Piketty's much-noted *Capital in the Twenty-First Century*, a rare example of an economics book with more than eight hundred pages that became a bestseller. Piketty talks about the world returning to a system of "patrimonial capitalism," where much of the economy is dominated by inherited wealth. He fears this is turning our society into an oligarchy, a place where a small group wields much more control over society than was ever expected in a democracy.

Another popular book, *Dream Hoarders: How the American Upper Middle Class Is Leaving Everyone Else in the Dust, Why That Is a Problem, and What to Do About It* by Richard Reeves, shows how inherited wealth impacts a lot more than the total sum of the next generation's assets. Wealth provides many early life advantages, particularly high-quality education, further ensuring that wealthy parents are able to pass on their status to their children. Reeves argues that this creates a "rigged market" for opportunity, less social mobility, and a less competitive economy. Furthermore, when children from wealthy families succeed, they (and society) may attribute more of their success than is warranted to their innate talents and hard work, rather than to the better schools, private tutoring, additional enrichment, and networking opportunities "hoarded" by wealthier families. The more people underestimate the importance of these advantages, the less they may feel compelled to support policies to make such advantages available to children from a wider range of backgrounds.

The founders of our nation did not address the risk that democratically elected representatives would allow the interests of a small minority of the population, such as the wealthy, to get too far ahead of the interests of the great majority. They believed that any elected representatives who allowed this to happen would be voted out of office. In fact, they raised almost the exact opposite concern: that in a democracy, the majority might trample the rights of the minority. Specifically, they were concerned that the majority would vote to tax away the wealth of the much less numerous rich. The Electoral College is one of the things we are saddled with as a result of this concern.

But unlike the founders, we all know how money has distorted the political process. As much as some may like to think of voters as making well-informed decisions based on enlightened self-interest, money talks and voters seem to listen and follow. This is especially true since the Supreme Court opened the floodgate to allow essentially unlimited corporate money to be spent on influencing elections in 2010 with the *Citizens United* case, which we'll discuss in chapter 8. I'll leave the topic of how and why we can be so easily manipulated by politicians with huge amounts of cash to the books on political science. The fact that we can, and its consequences, is what's important here.

Increasing wealth concentration, and the income and power that comes with it, usually does not end well. Throughout history, great inequality of wealth has often resulted in violent revolution (such as the French, Chinese, and Russian Revolutions) or national collapse (such as the fall of Rome). Occasionally, a particularly virulent plague came along and reordered society (such as the bubonic plague in medieval Europe). The good news is that those outcomes can be avoided.

The final two chapters of this book discuss government policies that can achieve the key goal of reducing inequality while promoting productivity. In particular, the last chapter discusses our tax system and shows how it makes a bad situation worse—how taxes actually worsen economic inequality—and what can be done to reverse that. The benefit of waiting until the end of the book to have that discussion is that by the time you get to it, you'll have the background knowledge to assess which ways would work best.

In the next chapter, we look beyond our borders to the rest of the world to see the global effect on us and our economy.

THE (MOSTLY) OPEN ECONOMY

What Are the Consequences of International Trade?

> Free trade, one of the greatest blessings which a government can confer on a people, is in almost every country unpopular.
>
> —Thomas B. Macaulay, British historian and politician

WHY HAVE FREE TRADE IN THE FIRST PLACE?

Free trade refers to the ability to buy goods and services from other nations (imports) and to sell goods and services to other nations (exports). The amount of trade in America and almost all nations isn't something directly determined by the government. It's the result of billions of individual decisions by Americans to buy something foreign made, and billions of individual decisions by individuals abroad to buy something American made.

Many Americans see a virtue in buying goods made in the United States. They believe that buying domestic strengthens the U.S. economy and creates jobs for Americans. Putting aside the issue of whatever "made in America" means in a world where many goods contain components made and then assembled in several different nations, is this in fact a virtue? Should people forgo cheaper or better foreign products to buy American-made products?

Consumers benefit when they buy goods made abroad. How do I know that? If they didn't, they wouldn't have bought the foreign goods in the first place. If a local manufacturer could make a product that a consumer preferred to the foreign product, the consumer would have bought the local product. In addition, since the price of the local choice benefits from cheaper and more efficient delivery, there is a good chance that the consumer had more than a slight preference for the foreign choice.

For example, Bangladesh has a great climate for growing mangoes and abundant labor to harvest them, so Europeans buy mangoes from Bangladesh, rather than going to the great expense and difficulty of trying to grow and harvest mangoes in Europe. The cost of growing mangoes in Bangladesh and then shipping them to Europe is less than the cost of growing them in Europe. How do I know that? Using the same logic that I used in the last paragraph: If it weren't cheaper to grow mangoes in Bangladesh, people would be growing them in Europe rather than importing them. Similarly, Europe is home to a large number of aerospace engineers and quality aviation infrastructure, so Bangladeshis buy airplanes from Europe rather than going to the great expense and difficulty of building an airplane on their own.

Bangladesh's ability to produce mangoes at a lower cost than Europe and Europe's ability to produce airplanes at a lower cost than Bangladesh is called a "comparative advantage." Comparative advantage doesn't mean that the other nation cannot make the product. It doesn't even mean that the other nation cannot make the product well. It just means that the nation with the comparative advantage can make the product less expensively than the other nation, so it pays to buy the product from them. Every nation has a comparative advantage in something due to their climate, natural resources, or, simply, inexpensive labor. Americans *could* assemble phones, sew generic clothing, and manufacture televisions, but other nations, such as China, can do those tasks at a significantly lower cost. Therefore, it pays for us to buy those goods from them.

The gains from free trade are so abundant—not only lower-priced products, but also access to a wider variety of goods and services and closer links to other nations and cultures—that the wealth of a nation and its openness to trade have historically been strongly linked to each other. For example, in the thirteenth through fifteenth centuries, Venice was the world's largest and most important center of trade connecting Western Europe with the Byzantine Empire and the Muslim world. Even today, people flock there to see the many vestiges of how wealthy, vibrant, and interesting it was. Similarly, seventeenth-century Amsterdam was one of the world's great centers of trade, and its "Golden Age" still animates the city. The wealth the Dutch created enabled them to explore the globe and set up a trading outpost in North America. That small colony took advantage of its natural harbor in the new country to become one of the world's great trading centers and, in turn, one of the richest and most diverse cities of all time (while changing its name to "New York City" along the way).

While the benefits from international trade in rich nations may be more conspicuous, the benefits in poor nations are significant and fall mostly into two categories. First, people in poorer nations get access to goods that they might have trouble producing on their own at any price, such as airplanes, computer equipment, and, for better or worse, advanced armaments. Second, many of them get additional job opportunities since what they export, such as inexpensive clothes and relatively simple manufactured products, typically requires a lot of labor. These jobs may not pay much, but they can provide a relatively better alternative for many workers.

In some less-developed nations, however, the opportunity to give people the first step on a ladder to a better life has been hijacked. Many businesses, particularly manufacturers, maintain unsafe and deplorable working conditions, pollute the environment, and destroy children's lives by employing them when they should be in school gaining a chance to better themselves and their community. Such businesses take advantage of the desperation facing many people in these nations and exploit them for higher profits.

If this sounds familiar, it should, since we have already discussed a very similar situation—the beginning of the Industrial Revolution. I called life in the early factories "probably the worst conditions people who were not expressly being punished or enslaved had ever endured." Some people today may be consoled by how much life has improved in the developed world and assume that workers in the less-developed world will achieve the same outcome in the long run. Nevertheless, as the economist John Maynard Keynes famously said, "In the long run, we are all dead."

Whether such difficult conditions had to be endured in the early days of the Industrial Revolution in order to build an economy where the average person in developed nations today has access to abundant food, decent housing, and a wide range of life-improving goods and services is debatable. Whether such difficult conditions need to be endured today is not. The world is a much, much richer place now than it was in the early days of the Industrial Revolution and there is no reason workers should suffer today the way they did then. As a point of reference, if we divided total world GDP (approximately $84.7 trillion in 2020[1]) evenly among all of the world's people (approximately 7.8 billion people[2]), the result for a family of four would be $43,426—enough so that no one on the planet would live in poverty.

As a practical matter, the added cost of providing humane and safe working conditions would add little to the cost of imported products. If a product makes sense to import now rather than produce domestically, a few improvements in working conditions is unlikely to significantly change that conclusion. Wealthy nations can insist that all businesses meet certain basic minimum standards, forgo child labor, and provide humane working conditions.

If a nation regularly fails to enforce such rules, the rest of the world can impose penalties on the nation or, in extreme cases, threaten to cut off trading with them to get them to act. That way, developing nations are not just incented to adopt some basic standards (which, to varying degrees, they are today), but to actually enforce them (which they often aren't today).

Free trade has the potential to enable the people of each nation to vastly expand the market for their goods and services and, thereby, empower them and their children to build better lives. We should not allow businesses that abuse workers, despoil the environment, and exploit children to deny the world's most desperate people that opportunity. These workers should not have to wait two hundred years (roughly the time from the start of the Industrial Revolution to the establishment of a robust middle class in the West) to have a better life.

WHAT HAPPENS TO MONEY SPENT ON IMPORTS?

One of the key themes of this book is that the fundamental principles of economics should become clear if you're willing to carefully observe the world and apply common sense. This is true of the global economy as well. As we discussed, U.S. currency (the dollar) and the currencies of virtually every other nation are fiat currencies—money created out of thin air by governments. Each one-dollar bill costs our government approximately 6.2 cents to make, and each higher-denomination bill costs between 10.8 and 14.0 cents to make (since those bills contain more security features).[3]

Is there a problem with all of us opting to work a few hours a year, printing green slips of paper that cost us several cents each, and then trading them for goods and services worth many, many times that amount? Are imports the ultimate free lunch? You may be thinking the problem with simply creating new money for this purpose is that it would cause inflation. Nevertheless, as you know, if new money results in new goods and services—and imports definitely result in new goods and services for our economy in an amount equal to the amount of the new money—prices are not affected. So, can we just print money to buy everything we need or want from abroad?

The answer becomes clear if you think about what happens to that money when it lands in the hands of the foreigners who sold us the French wine, the Swiss watch, or the Chinese everything. They may use those dollars to buy things from us. Or they may hold those dollars for a while and *then* use them to buy things from us. Or they may exchange those dollars at some bank or currency-exchange office that will hold those dollars until another customer needs them to buy things from us. Or the dollars may change hands many times abroad before they ultimately wind up in the hands of someone who wants to buy things from us. What do all of these scenarios have in common? They all result in the dollars that are spent abroad eventually being re-spent in the United States.

It may take a while for dollars spent on French wine today to come back, but there were dollars spent abroad years ago for French wine that are coming back today. Every day, we send some dollars abroad to buy imports, and foreigners send some dollars back to buy our exports. If each dollar did not give foreigners the right to claim a dollar's worth of goods and services in the United States, then the foreigners would not have had much interest selling us stuff for dollars in the first place.

How many dollars are abroad? While we know that approximately $2.21 trillion in U.S. currency is in circulation,[4] we have no way of knowing how much of that amount is held abroad. Currency is simply paper—it doesn't have any sort of embedded tracking device. Nevertheless, analysts who have looked at this issue estimate that approximately 60 percent to 70 percent of our national currency is held abroad.[5] Why so much? The U.S. dollar is considered a very safe and liquid asset, meaning its value is immediately recognized and accepted throughout the world.

Therefore, it's an alluring store of value to many people and institutions, particularly in more volatile nations.

Clearly, there are some dollars that left the United States to pay for imports and have not been re-spent back in the United States. This actually represents a gain for Americans. We traded money we created out of thin air for stuff with real value. When our imports exceed our exports, we got more goods and services from the rest of the world than they got from us. So, why is this a bad thing? Why do many people complain about our "trade deficit"?

The first step in figuring out what problem, if any, is caused by the "trade deficit" is to know what the term means. It simply means the amount by which the sale price of all the goods and services the United States imports exceeds the sale price of all the goods and services the country exports. In 2020, the United States imported $2.77 trillion of goods and services from abroad and exported $2.12 trillion of goods and services.[6] This created a $650 billion "trade deficit" for that year. The United States typically runs a trade deficit, although the one for 2020 was above average.

You may at this point be wondering, how can there regularly be a trade deficit of this magnitude if, as we discussed, most of the money we spend abroad is re-spent in the United States? The answer is that the trade deficit only accounts for spending on "goods and services." It does not take into account spending on assets and investments, such as purchases of shares in or bonds issued by American corporations, loans to Americans, purchases of U.S. government bonds, and acquisitions of U.S. real estate. When all of these asset purchases and investments are taken into account, the amount of money leaving America is essentially the same as the amount of money coming back into America.* We may import more goods and services than we export, but we export more assets and investments than we import.

---

* If the relatively small change in the amount of dollars held abroad is taken into account and some other minor technical adjustments are made, the amount we spend on imports and investments abroad equals the amount foreigners spend on our exports and investments in America.

Any dollars that fail to come back to the United States as purchases of goods, services, assets, or investments and instead stay abroad as reserves for foreign financial institutions, businesses, and, not insignificantly, corrupt officials represent a one-time gain to our economy. We traded money that was created out of thin air for real goods and services. The Fed could simply increase our money supply to compensate for any dollars that permanently leave our economy.

The dollars lost to some foreign vault could be replaced with new dollars without any fear of inflation since the amount of money actually circulating in the economy would not be increased. Replacing the dollars that remain abroad doesn't cause inflation for the same reason that replacing worn-out bills with newly printed ones, which the government regularly does, doesn't cause inflation. The newly printed dollars just replace the dollars that have gone away—in one case, because they were shredded by the government and in the other case, because they were stuffed in some dictator's vault for them and their heirs. As we'll discuss in chapter 11, the Fed always has the ability to adjust the number of dollars, both up and down, as needed.

Therefore, if almost all the dollars we spend abroad get re-spent in the United States and any dollars that stay abroad represent a gain to the United States, why do some people worry about the trade deficit and object to foreign trade? Who, in the words of the critics of free trade, is getting "ripped off" and how? Critics always say that jobs are lost and workers are hurt. But is that really the case?

TRADE AND JOBS

The answer to the question of whether trade hurts workers depends on who you are. If you are a low-skilled worker in the United States, the answer is a definitive "yes." Free trade is a big problem. Even at just $7.25 an hour, the current minimum wage in the United States, an American factory worker would have a hard time competing with a worker in Bangladesh, Vietnam, or even China, where the average hourly wage for a factory worker is significantly less. For example, in India—a nation with no shortage of potential workers—salaries for low-level factory work average less than $1 per hour.[7] Furthermore, as previously discussed, even though many low-skilled jobs (like housekeeping, cleaning, and delivery jobs) cannot be moved abroad, many can be fully or partially, increasing the competition and decreasing the pay for those jobs that remain in America. Therefore, low-skilled American workers have been, to use a technical term that most books on economics avoid, screwed by international trade.

On the other hand, for most people, international trade has led to significant benefits. We may be aware of the less-expensive goods we get, but we are less likely to think about the greater income and job opportunities many of us receive as a result of trade. How many extra workers are there at Microsoft because of their software sales abroad? How many extra professors are there at American universities because of the many international students who come here to study? How many extra employees are there at Goldman Sachs because the company provides investment products globally? How many extra copies of this book will be sold because it's available abroad? (The last one may not be the best example.)

The person who loses their job to a worker located in a different country is very much aware of their loss and the reason for it. Their unemployment or underemployment may be a source of bitterness or anger. Their plight is regularly depicted in the media and is the subject of several best-selling books. Their increased death rate due to suicide, alcoholism, and drug addiction has attracted so much attention that it even has a name: deaths of despair.

As I am sure you can guess, free trade not only exacerbates the winner-take-all trend with regard to individuals, but also extends this trend to entire communities. Places like Seattle and San Francisco are becoming even wealthier than they would have otherwise because of free trade. On the other hand, places that relied on manufacturing, like Detroit and Cleveland, are getting hit hard. Being on the losing end of this trend is awful, but, as we discussed, being on the winning end of the winner-take-all phenomenon is not as great as it sounds. The wealthiest cities in America are struggling with unaffordable housing, homelessness, and less vibrant street life as more housing gets snapped up by residents who are rarely there because they have multiple homes. This is not just a problem for these people and these communities—it's a problem for all of us when our nation fails to live up to its potential.

The larger group of people who gain in significant ways (like engineers or entertainers) and in less significant ways (like me) are not as aware of the additional demand for the work they do because some of what they produce gets sold abroad. They generally attribute their success to their own skills and hard work. They may be totally unaware that they would probably be less successful if Americans were not able to sell their products in foreign markets, which make up approximately 75 percent of total world spending.[8]

So, what's the net result of free trade in goods and services for the United States? On one hand, we lose low-skill jobs because we import a lot of cheap manufactured products due to the abundance of inexpensive labor abroad. On the other hand, we gain high-skill jobs because we export a lot of high-value products that take significant talent to make due to the abundance of advanced technical expertise in our nation.

It's almost impossible, however, to calculate exactly how many jobs we lose and how many we gain. For example, while the number of jobs at Microsoft due to foreign sales can be estimated, estimating all the jobs created by the spending of those extra Microsoft employees (at restaurants, private schools, retail shops, and countless other places) is very difficult. Even more difficult to estimate is the extra spending (and thus job creation) due to the additional expenditures by all those restaurant, private school, and retail shop employees that the extra Microsoft employees patronize. The new jobs and income created by exports creates multiple rounds of new jobs and spending in, what economists call, a "multiplier" effect. At the same time, the lower spending of the workers who lost jobs due to imports has a *negative* multiplier effect. These workers spend less, and that cut in spending also ripples through the economy.

Many politicians and labor activists assume international trade destroys more low-paid jobs than it produces high-paid jobs, for a net loss of American jobs. Why? Because we import more goods and services than we export, and selling investments and assets creates few jobs. Furthermore, what we do import tends to involve more workers (in other words, is more labor-intensive) than what we export. Some recent research suggests, however, that trade does not result in a net loss of jobs due to the multiplier effect.[9] Specifically, with the increase in the number of high-paid jobs comes an increase in spending and an increase in the number of service jobs.

The bottom line is that free trade gives us access to a cheaper and wider selection of products and our nation gains some high-skill, high-paying jobs, and loses some low-skill, low-paying jobs. So, free trade is great, unless you're one of the workers whose skills were rendered obsolete or you live in a community with a key industry that was rendered obsolete.

RESPONSES TO JOB LOSS

Since free trade has such significant material benefits and increases interaction and cooperation among nations, the question should not be whether to abandon free trade, but how we can distribute its benefits more equitably. One clear solution is that the larger group of free trade winners (those thriving in the global economy) could compensate the smaller group of free trade losers (those who have lost their jobs due to foreign competition and lack the skills to obtain new ones). That way, everyone could come out ahead.

Specifically, the government could offer free technical or higher education, training programs for new jobs, enhanced unemployment benefits, early retirement options, or even government jobs for displaced workers, all paid for by a small increase in taxes on the large number of people who are thriving in the open economy. It *could* do that, but it hasn't. Instead, we have a growing class of people burning mad about foreigners "taking our jobs" while many politicians sit by and watch it all happen or exploit the anger for their own political advantage. At the same time, many of us who have benefitted from international trade rarely think about what those benefits are, how great they are, or how they came about. At the risk of understatement, this is not a situation that makes for good public policy or for the election of the best candidates to public office.

One of the policy responses to the concern about the effect of free trade on jobs has been tariffs. Tariffs are simply taxes imposed by the government on imports. (They can be charged either as a fixed amount on each imported item or as a percentage of the imported item's price, like a sales tax.) Although certain proponents of tariffs claim otherwise, tariffs are not paid by the foreign manufacturers of imported goods. Foreign companies located abroad don't pay U.S. taxes and aren't subject to the jurisdiction of the U.S. tax code. Instead, the U.S.-based importer pays the tariff due to our government when they bring the imported goods into this country. Importers are intermediaries who pay for the imports and then charge the cost of the goods, all of their related expenses (including the tariffs), and some margin of profit for their efforts to the U.S. retailer who in turn sells the goods to us. The bottom line: You and I get stuck paying the tariff, not some foreign company.

Since tariffs make imported goods more expensive, they give an advantage to domestic producers of alternative goods. For example, if I prefer a French wine over a similar California wine and they both cost $20 per bottle, I will buy the French wine. If the government imposes a 30 percent tariff on French wine, the cost of the French wine to me, the consumer, goes up by the amount of the tariff, to $26. I may therefore switch to the $20 California wine. This sounds good for California wineries and their employees, but it's bad for consumers. They either have to pay more for the French wine they like or pay the same $20 for the California wine that they like less. It's also very bad for Boeing, Netflix, Microsoft, New York University, and so many other domestic entities and their employees that rely on spending by foreigners for support. Remember, if foreigners cannot earn dollars by selling things to us, they cannot spend dollars buying things from us.

The more goods on which tariffs are imposed and the higher the tariffs, such as in a "trade war" where nations keep increasing their tariffs to retaliate against each other, the more consumers lose. Furthermore, since the imported goods just went up in price due to the tariff (remember the cost of the French wine went from $20 to $26), the domestic producer feels less pressure to keep prices low, keep quality high, and stay competitive with the foreign producer. That California winery could now probably raise the price of their wine a few dollars or not make as much of an effort regarding quality and not lose much business. As a result, I would have to pay more for wine I like less or simply decide to buy fewer things—neither of which is a great outcome for me or for our nation.

The effect of tariffs on producers is also bad. The producers of less-preferable domestic products (like the California winery in the example above) are rewarded, while the producers of the products that Americans excel at producing, the ones that the entire world wants to purchase, are hurt. When Americans cut back on imports, fewer dollars flow to the foreigners who want to buy the internationally competitive goods and services America produces, like airplanes, big-budget films, music, and financial services. This is not a recipe for promoting the competitiveness of America's businesses and, therefore, the health of the American economy.

You may remember that President Trump once said, "Trade wars are good, and easy to win." As with most wars, however, they cause a great deal of very bad things to happen. Human life may not be lost as in a real war, but value for American consumers, opportunities for America's most competitive businesses, and jobs for America's most skilled employees *are* all lost. Moody's Analytics has estimated that the escalation in tariffs under President Trump reduced our GDP by approximately $65 billion and cost us 300,000 jobs.[10]

Going to "war" is almost always the costliest and least constructive way to respond to a problem. If China or some other trading partner steals our intellectual property or violates the rules of international trade in some other way, the World Trade Organization (WTO), which was established for this very purpose, can adjudicate the dispute. The United States was instrumental in establishing the WTO, and China, as well as the vast majority of world's nations, are members. If the remedies the WTO imposes are inadequate, the answer is not to give up on it. The answer is to improve it so that it can accomplish its mission of ensuring compliance with trade agreements and promoting free and fair trade. Old-fashioned diplomacy and coordinated pressure from trading partners can also help address such a situation. When we have a problem with a trading partner, war, whether it be a hot one, a cold one, or a trade one, should be the last resort, not the first.

We now turn back to the domestic economy to discuss how America's businesses, the entities responsible for producing our goods and services, are organized, owned, and valued. We'll also discuss what drives them, what influences them, and how the winner-take-all phenomenon is affecting them.

Part III

BUSINESS

7

THE PRIVATE SECTOR AND THE STOCK MARKET

How Is Business Organized, Owned, and Valued?

If stock market experts were so expert, they would be buying stock, not selling advice.

—Norman Ralph Augustine, chairman and CEO of Lockheed Martin

WHAT ARE CORPORATIONS?

As long as there have been people, there has been business. Those who specialized in hunting and gathering food traded with those who specialized in sewing together animal skins, and the division of labor and specialization presumably made both better off as a result. As time went on, trading and business activity expanded and often became more complicated and expensive. In particular, around the 1400s, world exploration took off. Building, outfitting, and launching an expedition to explore the world and bring back goods and resources that were found abroad was hugely expensive. The cost combined with the great risk involved made it unlikely that one person or a small group of people would be both able and willing to take on such a project. As a result, corporations came into being.

A corporation is an organization set up by law for the purpose of conducting business and producing goods and services.* Although corporations are not actual people, corporations are treated as distinct entities for almost all purposes. Specifically, they are treated as distinct and separate from their owners, also known as shareholders.

To see how a corporation is owned, you can envision a pie divided into even slices. In the case of a corporation, these slices are called shares. If the corporation has 100 shares outstanding (in other words, owned by shareholders)† and a shareholder owns one share, they own 1 percent of the corporation. Since all of the shares have the same value, the total value of the company is simply the share price times the number of shares outstanding. For example, as of this writing, the most valuable company in the world is Apple Inc. Its ownership is divided into approximately 16.4 billion shares valued at $171 each, giving it a total value of just over $2.8 trillion.

Shareholders get one vote for each share they own on major business decisions, such as whether to merge with another company, whether to move the company abroad, and whether to dissolve the company. Corporations also, from time to time, decide to distribute some of their profits to their shareholders (by declaring regular or onetime dividends) rather than retain them in the company, and shareholders share in dividends in proportion to the number of shares they own.

---

* There are also non-profit corporations set up for the purpose of providing various types of public benefits. The discussion in this chapter concerns only for-profit corporations.

† Corporations often own some of their own shares. These "treasury shares" do not convey any ownership interest and aren't entitled to dividends or voting rights. As a practical matter, it's as if those shares don't exist.

CORPORATIONS, LIMITED LIABILITY, AND FAIRNESS

Anyone can conduct business and produce goods and services without forming a corporation. They can also join with others to do so in what is called a partnership. So why is almost every significant business a corporation? Limited liability for the corporation's owners is the big reason.

The filing of a state incorporation form and the payment of a couple-hundred-dollar fee turns a business into a corporation, allowing its owners (now called "shareholders") to be free from any personal liability or harm caused by the corporation. So, if you, along with your business partners, owned an oil tanker that leaked and spilled 10.8 million gallons of oil over 1,300 miles of pristine coastline, you would be personally liable for the billions of dollars in cleanup costs. If you, along with your fellow *shareholders*, owned this ill-fated oil tanker (let's call it the *Exxon Valdez*) through a corporation, you would *personally* not owe one cent toward the cleanup costs. The protection from liability afforded by incorporating is why all but the very smallest businesses (such as the one-person business that cleans your home or mows your lawn) are organized as corporations.

The limited liability of corporations protects only the personal assets of the shareholders, not the corporation's own assets. The money and property owned by the corporation itself is still available to address any harm or liabilities the company causes. Clearly, when significant corporate assets are used to pay for the harm done, the value of the company's shares gets hit. The value of a share can actually be reduced to nothing, as the shareholders of Enron found out after all of Enron's crooked accounting was revealed and the company collapsed in 2001. Actions that greatly reduce or eliminate the value of a corporation's shares, like Enron's massive frauds, are often news to the shareholders just as they are to everyone else when they are finally disclosed. But a share's value can never go below zero, which means a shareholder can never lose more than what they paid for their shares.

Limiting the liability of a corporation's shareholders may seem somewhat unfair to those harmed by the corporation. Nevertheless, we might all be living like food-insecure peasants in medieval villages if not for corporations. Limited liability encourages investors—from the smallest and least sophisticated to the largest and savviest—to put up money for huge and risky enterprises that can change the world.

By incorporating and, thereby, turning their owners with unlimited personal liability into shareholders with limited liability, businesses were able to raise the vast sums needed to create efficient assembly lines, develop new drugs, construct the immense power plants needed to provide electricity, and build the infrastructure that makes the internet and smartphones a reality. Large essential companies could not have raised the many billions of dollars they needed if their owners feared getting hit with unlimited charges for any accident or other problem the company might have.

Holding shareholders personally liable for the actions of their companies would also raise a fairness concern. Many corporations are large and complex organizations. The shareholder pool is often too wide (there are too many shareholders) and too shallow (each of the many thousands of shareholders does not have a significant enough interest or ability to affect the corporation) for shareholders to take an active role in the business.

Therefore, every corporation is required to have a board of directors that oversees the company on behalf of its shareholders. The shareholders may vote for the directors, but the board of directors merely adds to the distance between the shareholders and their company. The directors select the company's chief executive officer (CEO) and delegate to them the day-to-day management of the company. The CEO selects the other manager/officers (like the president, chief financial officer, and general counsel). In sum, the managers report to the CEO, the CEO reports to the directors, and the directors are elected by the shareholders, putting significant distance between a large corporation's shareholders and the people making decisions on the corporation's behalf.

This distance means that the vast majority of shareholders are unlikely to be aware of the issues faced and actions taken by the corporation. (If you own shares in a company, how aware are you of the day-to-day actions and issues facing that company? Given the popularity of mutual funds, how aware are you of which companies' shares you even own?) Therefore, since the beginning of corporations in the 1400s, shareholders have been insulated from personal liability for the actions of a corporation.

So far, we have only talked about how limited liability affects the shareholders. How about how limited liability affects those who suffer harm? Specifically, is limiting the amount of compensation to those harmed by a corporation to whatever assets the corporation happens to have, fair? Why should someone burned by coffee at McDonald's have access to more compensation than someone burned by coffee at a small local coffee shop just because both are incorporated? For better or for worse, the law is supposed to treat all parties equally, regardless of their assets. A person who owns a share in the small coffee shop has the same protection from personally paying for any harm done as the millionaire who owns a share in McDonald's. What this means is that small business shareholders, who are more likely to be involved in the business, have the same protections as large business shareholders, who may not even be aware of the fact that they are shareholders.

So, if the shareholders are insulated from liability and the corporation itself is out of assets, is there any other source of funds for the victims of a corporation's harmful actions? In an ideal world, the answer would be yes. If the corporate executives, the people making the day-to-day decisions for the business, are acting with insufficient care for the public, maybe some of their own money should be on the line. Maybe they should pay for some of the harm they cause even *before* the shareholders get hit.

That is not, however, how it works. Any harm caused by a corporation is paid for with the corporation's assets. Therefore, the money only comes out of the shareholders' investment. While it's possible that a corporate employee's criminal activity could result in personal liability for harm they caused, that would be rare and unusual. For example, despite all the fraud and financial abuse in the mortgage industry that helped pave the way for the Great Recession of 2008, there was negligible personal liability for mortgage industry executives. Instead, their dishonest actions resulted in a great deal of new regulations. Who paid for the cost of complying with these new regulations? Primarily the shareholders, since greater costs reduce profits. To the extent the costs were passed on in higher prices for the corporation's products, consumers also paid. Most of the executives who caused the problems in the first place were off the hook.

Every single action a corporation takes, legal or illegal, is the action of a real-live human being employed by the company. Threatening the human being who acted illegally with significant fines or incarceration would be more effective at getting corporate employees to act with integrity than more regulation for their company and costs for their shareholders and, potentially, customers. Instead of indicting a corporation and hope it has some kind of effect on the executive responsible for the illegal act, prosecutors could indict the executive directly.

As the former general counsel of a major financial company, I can confirm what you already know—people are more likely to commit illegal acts when the benefit from them seems big and the downside seems small. Think of the innumerable mortgage brokers who helped falsify information on mortgage loan applications in order to qualify more people for loans and earn more commissions—they might have acted differently if the downside were a stint in prison rather than a slap on the wrist from their employer. Holding corporate executives to a lower standard when they act on behalf of their company than when they act on their own behalf in their personal life is asking for trouble.

Fortunately, all of us have ways to influence and change corporate behavior, and these are discussed in the next chapter. But before we get to that, we need to discuss how a corporation's share price, the focus of much attention, is determined.

CORPORATIONS AND THE STOCK MARKET

The vast majority of large corporations are "publicly" owned, which means that their shares can be bought and sold by any member of the public on a stock exchange (like the New York Stock Exchange). Therefore, you and I can join Mark Zuckerberg as an owner of Facebook, although our ownership percentage would be considerably smaller than his. To become public, a company must meet a formidable set of requirements imposed by the Securities and Exchange Commission, an agency of the federal government, and publicly release voluminous detailed information on its products, operations, and prospects.

If a company is not public, like most small companies and a few large ones like Bloomberg L.P. and Koch Industries, its shares are said to be "privately" owned. This means members of the public cannot become owners unless the company's existing shareholders agree to sell them shares in a private transaction. It also means that the company can avoid disclosing all the detailed information on its activities that public companies are required to disclose.

Who controls a corporation? If you own more than 50 percent of its outstanding shares, you do. That lets you win any shareholder vote. You can vote in a new slate of directors (which can include you) who will hire a new CEO (which can be you) who will change the direction of the company. If the corporation is large with thousands of shareholders, many of whom are not following what's going on or voting in elections, you can probably control it with much less than 50 percent. For example, Jeff Bezos owns 11.1 percent of the almost 500 million outstanding shares of Amazon,[‡] which is enough for him to control the company. (The next-largest individual shareholder owns 0.02 percent of Amazon's shares, and the largest institutional shareholder is a brokerage company that owns 7.1 percent of Amazon's shares.)

---

‡ Some of these shares may be owned by Jeff Bezos's immediate family members.

HOW IS SHARE PRICE DETERMINED?

The price of a corporation's shares is determined the way the price of most things is determined: by supply and demand. When people buy a share of a corporation, they are literally getting a share of the corporation and all of its future profits. So, if people think the company has good prospects, buyers will outnumber sellers and the company's share price will rise; if not, sellers will outnumber buyers and its share price will drop.

John Maynard Keynes once likened this process to a beauty contest that was run back in his day (in the early twentieth century) in which a newspaper offered a prize to the person who picked the six most-attractive women out of an array of photos. The twist? Attractiveness was based on everyone's selections, rather than on any formal criteria. Therefore, it didn't matter who were objectively the most attractive. All that mattered was who each contestant thought the other contestants would think were the most attractive. The stock market is similar—investors buy stocks they think other investors will buy. Keynes summed up the lesson by saying, "Successful investing is anticipating the anticipations of others."

Notwithstanding the claims of many investment advisors, there's no objective formula for identifying the most promising stocks, just as there's no objective formula for predicting the outcome of the beauty contest Keynes described. If there were, as the quote at the beginning of this chapter noted, those investment advisors would be cashing in big-time for themselves rather than spending their time trying to sell their ideas to you.

Business experts have come up with a theory to explain how the market arrives at share prices: the efficient markets hypothesis. The hypothesis states that each company's share price incorporates everyone's opinion on the future value of that company. For example, if two companies have similar current earnings but most people think one has greater prospects for the future, that company's stock price should be higher by the amount its prospects are expected to exceed the other company's prospects.

Support for this theory can be provided by dropping in on any investment bank where some of the smartest and most diligent recent college and business school graduates work as "analysts" spending their days (and nights and weekends) poring over company filings, market data, economic indicators, news articles, investor chat rooms, and countless other sources. What are they looking for? Companies whose stock price veers even slightly from what they think (based on everything they have read and heard) that value should be. Any deviation is an opportunity for their company (and for them) to make some money. If these analysts conclude that the stock price is too low, they will buy the stock with the expectation that its price will eventually rise to the value they think it should have. If they conclude the stock price is too high, they will sell the stock (or "short" the stock, which involves placing a bet that the stock price will fall). The net effect of this activity at investment banks and by many individual investors should be to push the price for each stock to a widely accepted fair value for the company.

This process is where the term "efficient market" comes from—stock prices should quickly and efficiently incorporate all public information regarding the company. I used the word "should" because what happens in the real world is, like in most cases, a lot messier than in the theoretical one. Investors (appearances sometimes to the contrary) are human beings, not machines—they often act impulsively, emotionally, and even irrationally. That is how "dot-com" stocks rose to extraordinary values (and subsequently crashed) in the euphoric early days of the internet and why "meme" stocks soar, because an obsession with them goes viral rather than because of any change in their business prospects.

Even when investors objectively and thoroughly assess information about a company, the valuation they reach can be greatly distorted because the publicly available information may not be complete or fully accurate. Furthermore, the information that is available is subject to manipulation by people with an interest in promoting the company (such as the company's management), as well as by people with an interest in demeaning the company (such as investors betting against the company's stock). Circulating false or misleading information about a company in order to influence its share price is, however, illegal. On the other hand, circulating a negative *opinion* about a company and its prospects is legal. The line between the two is not always clear and the government is reluctant to prosecute unless it is.

Someone who does have accurate information about a company that the rest of the public doesn't have, such as that a pharmaceutical company is about to come up with a blockbuster new drug, can make a lot of money. They can buy shares in the company and watch its price soar after the company announces the great news. Or they can sell shares in a company that is about to announce bad news. The latter is what Martha Stewart did with her shares of ImClone right before the company announced that the government would not approve its new cancer drug. As Martha Stewart learned, trading based on "material inside information" (in other words, key information that the general public does not yet know) is a crime and can land you in prison.

What's important to understand is that the many buyers and sellers in the market nudge the price of corporate shares (as well as every other asset, for that matter) to a price that reflects a general consensus, however imperfect, as to its value. Some people may think they can outsmart the market and identify instances where the market got the price wrong and profit when the market corrects itself. Some of the most diligent and sophisticated investors like Warren Buffett have pulled off this trick many times. But they are the exception. Consistently outsmarting the many analysts and investors carefully assessing the value of a share is a trick that is rarely successful.

What Is the Effect of Share Buybacks?

As of this writing, the total value of all shares in U.S. public companies is approximately $49 trillion.[1] You might be surprised to learn that, according to Goldman Sachs, the biggest buyer of the shares of most major companies are not individuals, mutual funds, or pension funds, but the companies themselves.[2] In the last few years, companies have spent trillions of dollars buying back their own shares from the public markets. Why?

In theory, companies buy back their shares after determining that they have cash (usually from profits they made) that they don't need for their business and therefore should be returned to the company's owners—its shareholders. How does buying back shares benefit the shareholders?

You can see how by recalling the analogy between a corporation and a pie. When a corporation buys its own outstanding shares, they disappear from the market and no longer represent ownership. Therefore, ownership of the corporation is divided among fewer shares. Just as dividing a pie into fewer slices increases the size of the slices, dividing a corporation into fewer shares increases the value of its shares. The company's profits are divided among a smaller number of shares, causing the profits per share to increase. And when profits per share increase, the share price increases.

Just like dividends, share buybacks transfer cash from a company to its owners. When a company buys the shares of those who wish to sell, it merely directs the cash to those shareholders who are no longer interested in the company. It eliminates their ownership interest, which results in their interest being divided up among the remaining shareholders.

Since the executives who decide to use corporate funds to buy the shares also personally own a substantial number of shares, their actions increase their wealth, often significantly. Is spending the corporation's money to buy back its own shares a prudent business decision or a dishonest manipulation of the share price?

Many members of Congress, financial commentators, and labor unions have criticized share buybacks. They believe that if a company holds on to money it has determined it doesn't need for its operations, rather than spends it on acquiring its own shares, the company might use the money to promote a more equitable economy. They could use the cash to increase wages, create jobs, improve working conditions, or fund corporate social-responsibility programs. Nevertheless, if management had any interest in those things or thought any of that made sense for the company, they would have already done it. Would stopping buybacks force them to reconsider?

If share buybacks are limited or made illegal, as some legislators have proposed, companies could simply return money to their shareholders through dividends. A dividend directly puts cash in each shareholder's pocket, unlike a share buyback, which increases the value of each remaining share. From the company's perspective, this can be viewed as half a dozen of one versus six of another—in both cases the money is moved from the company to its shareholders. From a shareholder's perspective, a dividend is a less desirable way of getting cash from the company. Dividends are taxed (though, as you might suspect, at a lower rate than many people's wages), unlike the increase in value of shares that are not sold, which is not taxed.

You may ask: So, why doesn't the government simply restrict dividends as well as share buybacks? The answer is that the government has to allow some way for shareholders to get money out of their companies. If not, investors would have little interest in putting money in companies in the first place. Who would invest money in a new company that needs funds to start up or in an existing company that needs funds to expand or innovate if money could only go into the company, but not out? If the government merely delayed the process by which cash can be given back to shareholders rather than restricted it entirely, the result would be a corporate America further bloated with cash, hardly the desired outcome.

What would happen to this cash until it could finally be returned to shareholders? Since corporate executives are always looking to increase profits, they would most likely seek to earn a return on this money by investing it (in the shares of other companies, bonds, or something else). That way, when they could finally return the cash to the shareholders, there would be more of it.

Inequality in America is a massive problem and it needs to be addressed. But forcing companies to invest cash they don't need rather than return it to their owners for them to invest or spend will do nothing to help. Our efforts to increase equity while promoting productivity need to be focused on effective ways to make the playing field more level rather than on symbolic issues. One way to start is to focus on what drives corporate behavior and how it can be influenced, the subject of the next chapter.

CORPORATE BEHAVIOR

What Drives Corporations, and How Can They Be Influenced?

There is one and only one social responsibility of business—to use its resources and engage in activities designed to increase its profits so long as it stays within the rules of the game.

—Milton Friedman, Nobel Prize–winning economist

WHAT IS THE GOAL OF A CORPORATION?

According to *Fundamentals of Corporate Finance*,[1] a popular and widely assigned college textbook on finance, "the goal of financial management in a corporation is to maximize the current value per share of the existing stock."* You could choose basically any modern text on corporate finance and find essentially the same statement.

In all fairness, that goal does incorporate a broad range of incentives that most other goals would not. If the goal of the corporation were to maximize current profits, there would be an incentive

---

* A business organized as a partnership would focus on the value of their partners' interests.

to lay off huge numbers of employees and neglect the company's assets, thereby inflating current profits but killing off the company in the long run. If the goal were to maximize sales, the company would wind up taking on unprofitable business, undermining its long-term financial health. If the goal were to provide or save local jobs that pay more than foreign ones, the company would have a hard time surviving against its less altruistic competitors. If the goal were to provide significant social benefits, the company could adopt a religious or ideologically inspired agenda that the CEO would like but might appall you or me.

The goal of maximizing shareholder value incorporates a wide variety of goals because, as we discussed, a corporation's share price reflects the market's consensus view of its long-term prospects for success. And success, as we know, depends on a wide variety of factors. If a corporation rips off its customers, its share value should take a hit due to the resulting lawsuits, fines, bad publicity, and lost business. If it prudently invests in great new products or helps its workers to become more productive, its share value should go up due to increased profitability.

All of that may make sense in theory, but you still may be questioning whether increasing shareholder value should be the sole goal of a corporation. Specifically, if a corporation can legally get away with polluting, paying less than a living wage, shipping jobs abroad, or making unsafe products, should it do those things if they would increase profitability? And if these concerns led corporations to abandon the sole goal of increasing shareholder value, what should the new goal or set of goals be, who should decide on what they are, how should their importance be ranked, how should their achievement be monitored, and how should they be enforced?

The difficulty of governing the innumerable decisions each corporation makes every day, the reasons for them, and the many effects they have has led to where we are today where share price is the guiding light. Corporations often, however, do give lip service to supporting the greater social good and do have relatively small budgets for "corporate social responsibility" programs. For example, in 2018, the world's five-hundred largest companies spent just under 1 percent of their profits (0.06 percent of their revenues) on these programs.[2] This is a small price to pay for good publicity and the ability to brag about how they are improving society. Nevertheless, the vast majority of decisions made by corporate managers reveal that maximizing shareholder value is their paramount concern.

At this point, you may be thinking about cooperative corporations that are owned by their workers or customers and that do focus on goals other than profits. That model can work well for a relatively small business owned and run by people with shared goals, such as paying higher wages, employing workers who for various reasons have difficulty getting jobs, or providing products for which there is a limited market. There is, however, a reason that these cooperative corporations are dwarfed by conventional corporations: Their goals are not more widely shared. At the risk of sounding cynical, the real world reveals that most people act like corporations: They may give lip service to loftier goals, but their actions imply something less altruistic. Most consumers shop based on price and quality and rarely seem willing to pay higher prices to boost wages or subsidize more obscure products. There is a reason Walmart is the largest grocer and Amazon is the largest retailer in the United States and the Park Slope Food Coop remains a single, beloved local store in Brooklyn.

Even though the vast majority of corporations do have profit as their goal, their actions in pursuit of that goal are, however, limited by law and regulation. A corporation is free to do what it thinks will increase its share price as long as it complies with the rules we as a society have enacted regarding the environment, safety, labor standards, consumer disclosures, and literally every aspect of business activity. Urging, demanding, petitioning, or lobbying companies to change their behavior may work in some cases, but it's a less effective strategy than amending these rules and forcing them to change. But before we discuss how to bring about this change, we need to discuss how corporate behavior is determined by the actual human beings who control them.

Corporate officers have a legal or "fiduciary duty" to act in the "best interests" of the corporation. This policy is called the "business judgment rule" and it imposes a very weak standard for the actions of corporate officers. Judges are very reluctant to second-guess the actions of officers when they are legally challenged. Generally, as long as corporate officers have some credible claim that they're acting in the corporation's best interests and aren't breaking the law, they are free to run the business as they see fit. Similarly, the company's board of directors rarely act as a real check on management since most directors are close cronies with the CEO and top management, identify with key executives due to similar career paths, and fear that challenging management could cause them to lose their lucrative and prestigious board seat.

Therefore, clear direction for management is not provided by the law because of the business judgment rule, by the directors because of their cozy relationship with management, or by the shareholders because of their distance from the operations of the company. So, who or what is guiding management? The share price. The further you go up the corporate hierarchy, the more closely compensation is linked to the price of the company's shares. This link can be through stock options, whereby officers get paid any increase in the price of the stock over a period of time, or by outright grants of stock that officers get to hold or sell at their discretion.[†] As a result, management tends to be laser focused on share price. At the top, the vast majority of compensation for CEOs and many key officers is directly linked to share price.

Linking compensation to share price ensures that management generally has the same interest as the shareholders and not some other interest like making their jobs as safe, lucrative, and cushy

---

† In private companies of significant size, an estimate of what the share price would be if the company were publicly traded is usually used.

as possible. It does, however, reinforce the focus on increasing the company's share price. And, in a perfect world, the goal of increasing share price should focus management on the long-term health of the company. It should discourage management, for example, from making decisions that would boost short-term profits but do long-term damage to the company. Unfortunately, we don't live in a perfect world.

Management has a powerful incentive to make things look as good as possible in the moment. The current quarter's profitability is a certain number that everyone assessing the stock market can analyze, plug into their algorithms, and use to determine a price for the stock. On the other hand, the long-term health of the company is far from certain, cannot be determined with any precision, and cannot be reduced to a specific set of verifiable numbers that the company's auditors can certify. The future is also much more subject to management spin. Therefore, in the real world, the goal of increasing share price is not as benign as it may seem in theory. It often leads corporate managers to take excessive risks or undermine workers (acts that management can sweep under the rug or spin away) in order to make headlines for increasing short-term profits.

When typical companies take excessive risks, the companies themselves are put at risk. When financial companies take excessive risks, the entire economy may be put at risk. Therefore, since our goal is to understand the economy, we need to look at this specific part of the private sector more closely.

WHAT IS THE ROLE OF THE FINANCIAL INDUSTRY?

Financial companies, such as commercial banks, investment banks, hedge funds, venture capital funds, and other financial firms, are like any other businesses in that they are owned by their individual shareholders and focus on shareholder value. They are, however, unlike most other businesses in that their activities have an outsize influence on the economy. In particular, financial companies are often blamed for exacerbating or actually causing recessions, such as the Great Recession of 2008.

We will discuss the unique and important role U.S. banks have in the Federal Reserve System's process of creating money in chapter 11. But banks have a larger role in the economy than just helping the Fed manage the money supply. Additionally, the financial sector as a whole is much larger than just the banks.

The Bureau of Economic Analysis (BEA), which is part of the United States Department of Commerce, calculates how much each type of business contributes to our economy.[3] The largest category by far, at almost $4.6 trillion (approximately 22 percent of our economy) is "finance, insurance, real estate, rental, and leasing." This is just this category's direct share of the economy. Its influence on the remaining 78 percent is considerable.

The BEA breaks this category down one level further, showing that "finance and insurance" alone accounts for approximately $1.8 trillion annually. What insurance companies do is fairly clear: They take payments, called premiums, from a large number of policyholders and pool them, so they can provide funds to any policyholder who suffers a loss covered by their policy. In fact, what businesses in most of the BEA's categories do is fairly clear. But what do businesses in the finance sector actually do?

Their most basic, important, and traditional role is to match the funds of those who have money they don't currently need with those who need money they don't currently have, making everyone better off in the process. Those who provide the money (the savers/investors) get a return on it (such as interest, dividends, and capital gains). Those who receive the money get to do whatever they want to do earlier than they otherwise could have, such as buy a home, start a business, or invent a new product. The rest of us benefit from the additional businesses, infrastructure, educations, and other beneficial investments the availability of loans makes possible.

There are three main groups in our economy that seek money through the financial sector: consumers (individuals like you and me), businesses, and the government (federal, state, and local). Each can get the extra money they want through debt. What exactly is "debt"?

Think of it this way: Eskimos have an unusually large number of words for snow, which says something about their way of life. Well, the English language has an unusually large number of words for debt, and that probably says something about our way of life. Debt can and does take many diverse forms, and its name may change depending on who is borrowing and for what purpose. Examples of debt include a loan note from a student borrower, an obligation to repay a line of credit to a business, a mortgage note requiring a homeowner to repay money borrowed to buy a home, and a government or U.S. Treasury bond obligating the government to pay a sum of money to the bond's owner.

The bottom line is that whatever it's called and whatever form it takes, all debt is simply money owed by one party to another party. It's usually accompanied by a document that spells out the detailed terms on which that money must be repaid—specifically how and when the borrower must repay the amount borrowed (the "principal") and the interest on that amount. That's essentially all there is to debt no matter what it's called or what form it takes.

Businesses have one additional way of getting money from savers/investors that consumers and the government do not: equity. Equity is another word for ownership of all or a percentage of a business and, as we discussed in the last chapter, it's represented by shares of stock. Only businesses can raise money through equity since, thankfully, savers/investors cannot have ownership of a person (slavery has been abolished) and cannot have ownership of a part of the government (at least as of this writing).

Businesses that need money can, therefore, choose to raise it through debt or equity. The imaginative people in the financial sector have expanded their options by creating a range of products that merge characteristics of debt and equity in every conceivable way—inventing countless hybrids with names like preferred stock, convertible bonds, warrants, and debt with an equity kicker. For example, preferred stock is like regular or common stock[‡] in that it gives partial ownership in the company that issued it, except that it is also like debt in that it usually has a right to receive regular payments (like interest) and does not give the owner voting rights in the company. A convertible bond is like debt in that its owner receives interest, but it also gives the owner the right to convert the debt into equity under certain circumstances. All of these financial products are designed to channel money from people who do not spend it to others who will. That is the traditional business of a financial company, which seems no more complex or esoteric than most other businesses.

The reason the question "What do financial companies do?" may have seemed difficult to answer a few paragraphs back is because in recent decades, the quest for revenue, profit, and a higher share price has led financial companies to venture far beyond their traditional role. These companies have launched new mind-bogglingly complex products and instruments that have nothing at all to do with channeling money from people who do not spend it to others who will. Many of these products are designed to allow people to make bets on the financial performance of others, on specific financial indicators (such as future inflation or interest rates), or on almost anything.

For example, you can bet IBM's stock price is going up with a product called a "call option." You can bet Apple's stock price is going down with a product called a "put option." You can bet that the price of oil is going up with a product called a "futures contract." And last, but far from least, you can bet that a particular bundle of mortgage loans will pay off (or not pay off) with a product called a "credit default swap." Investment bankers can be extraordinarily creative in structuring these bets and giving them very impressive and intimidating names, such as the one at the end

---

‡ All other discussions of stock in this book refer to common stock. The convention is to use the term "stock" for common stock, unless the context requires clarification.

of the last sentence. Nevertheless, they're all essentially bets and they're all called "derivative securities" (or simply "derivatives") because they derive their value from something else—specifically, whether the subject of the bet happens or doesn't happen.

If this sounds like gambling, it's because that's precisely what it is. So how did this new role for financial companies develop?

Derivatives were originally designed to permit investors to reduce risk in their investment portfolios by hedging or, in other words, lessening their exposure to particular losses. For instance, if an investor owned a large amount of bonds issued by the city of Philadelphia, they would be concerned that Philadelphia could not or would not repay the bonds (put simply, that Philadelphia would default). Such an investor could protect him- or herself from loss by using a "credit default swap," which is actually very similar to an insurance policy. They would bet that Philadelphia would default by paying a fee (similar to an insurance premium) to another party who had more confidence in Philadelphia.

If Philadelphia *didn't* default, the other party would keep the fee and the investor would get all the money owed under the bonds from Philadelphia. If Philadelphia *did* default, the other party would have to reimburse the investor for all or a part (depending on the amount of the bet) of the loss the investor sustained (similar to an insurance company reimbursement for a loss). That way, although the investor would lose money due to the default by Philadelphia, they would make up at least some of the loss because they won their bet. For this reason, the law specifically permitted derivatives despite the fact that most states prohibit gambling (except for government lotteries, which are specifically allowed and, not coincidentally, earn states large amounts of money).

What started out as a tool—one that worked like insurance and enabled investors to manage risk—has morphed into a virtual casino, the size of which would make Las Vegas look insignificant. The number and complexity of the bets has grown exponentially and the vast majority seem to have nothing to do with investors protecting themselves from particular losses. The Bank for International Settlements estimated that the total amount of derivatives was $607 *trillion* in 2020.[4] It also estimated that the amount of credit default swaps, just one type of derivative, was $9 trillion. Even if these estimates are way off, their gigantic size demands attention.

Creating, marketing, executing, and monitoring these derivatives has become an enormous business and a source of significant profit for the financial sector. The institutions that engage in this business also attract some of the brightest people with the best educations. The obvious question is: How does the larger society benefit from all this, if at all?

For the vast majority of businesses, from manufacturers to service providers, the benefit from their products is clear. Even if you would never buy a particular product yourself, there is someone else who would and, as we discussed in chapter 2, presumably they got more benefit from the product than it cost them or they wouldn't have bought the product in the first place.

With derivatives, however, any amount gained by a customer who won a bet is matched by a loss for another customer who lost the bet. Therefore, derivatives may seem like a zero-sum game. However, derivatives are actually *less* than a zero-sum game for the customers because the financial sector siphons off fees in connection with structuring and arranging them. So, the answer to how society benefits from derivatives is the same as the answer to how society benefits from gambling in general. In moderation, these activities can be engaging and pose little harm. In excess, however, they produce immense harm that can greatly outweigh their entertainment value.

What kind of harm do derivatives pose? The sheer size of the market, along with how it employs such a large share of America's best and brightest, gives us a clue. The people engaged in this business could be seeking solutions to major problems, inventing useful new products, or curing diseases rather than devising hypercomplex bets that can destabilize the entire economy. This happened in 2008 when many billions of dollars of bets on the performance of mortgage loans went bad. Several major financial institutions, like Lehman Brothers, went bankrupt as a result, undermining faith in our financial system and our economy. The financial difficulty spread to the real economy, brought on the Great Recession, and did damage that was disproportionate to any possible benefit these derivatives could offer.

The derivatives market is another example of how economic inequality distorts the economy and increases volatility. If wealth and income were more evenly distributed, many of the resources devoted to this immense gambling operation for those with massive capital would be deployed elsewhere—presumably, somewhere that caused less harm and provided greater benefit.

We also see a similar distortion in a related area—as of this writing, money is pouring into alternative currencies, one of the financial sector's latest innovations (if you're willing to define the "financial sector" broadly). Speculation on alternative currencies, like most forms of speculation, is also very similar to gambling. The price of an asset, whether it's a Bitcoin, an NFT, or a meme stock, is bid up simply because people expect investors flush with cash will continue to bid it up. (There is much more about speculative "bubbles" in chapter 10.) Speculation on assets is not like traditional investing in business that generally creates real value by providing the funds needed to produce more goods and services, expand the economy, and thereby produce a return for the investor.

If people want to gamble, they can go to Las Vegas, rather than engage in a multitrillion-dollar activity that can disrupt the entire economy. In the same way that we have rules for the rest of the gambling industry, we need to limit the size, reach, and effects of the much larger derivatives market as well as any form of speculation that is measured in the trillions of dollars. Otherwise, we risk derailing the economy, as we did in 2008. As with trains, every effort should be made to keep the economy on track so as to avoid the much greater effort needed to get it back on track after having fallen off.

CHANGING CORPORATE BEHAVIOR

We've now discussed what motivates the people who call the shots in corporations generally and at financial companies in particular. What can we do if we're not happy with the results?

Influencing Corporate Behavior

Although corporations aren't people, they are very concerned with their images since, in many cases, their images or brands are among their most valuable assets. They are also run by people and are, therefore, sensitive to public criticism and ostracism, including targeted protests or boycotts. After all, a large protest or boycott might lead to a public relations nightmare, the loss of business, and an impaired share price. Such actions have worked in the past—today, there is less testing of cosmetics on animals, fewer genetically modified foods, and fewer harmful pesticides as a result.

You would think that since consumers who are troubled by a corporation's actions can organize, the shareholders of a corporation could organize even more easily. Since shareholders own their companies and many don't actually want them to poison groundwater, export jobs, and so on, why don't we see more change initiated by shareholders? Because organizing shareholders is actually very difficult.

As previously discussed, public companies may have hundreds of thousands of shareholders and there's no way of knowing who they are since public companies don't maintain lists of shareholders. In fact, most people own their shares of public companies in "street name," which means their broker's name or some other institution's name is listed as the owner. The listed owner owns or holds the shares for the benefit of the actual owner. Listing the broker or some other institution as the owner makes transferring sold shares much easier, since the broker can complete the paperwork for the transfer without involving the actual owner.

This process may be efficient, but it hides who actually owns the corporation's shares, even from the corporation itself. (If you own stock in a brokerage account, your stock is almost certainly held in street name. The corporation has no idea you own those shares.)

Furthermore, mutual funds, pension funds, and other institutions own approximately 80 percent of all shares,[5] and the real human beneficiaries of those shares are equally opaque. Finally, many, if not most, shareholders own stock in multiple companies, so their interest in any particular one is generally small.

The law does provide mechanisms whereby shareholders can directly influence their company's behavior. First, all shareholders can vote for new directors. Additionally, each public company shareholder who has owned at least $2,000 worth of the company's shares for at least three years, $15,000 worth of the shares for at least two years, or $25,000 of the shares for at least one year has the right to include *one* proposal in the annual mailing the company sends to its shareholders.[6] (For shares held in street name, the corporation sends the annual mailing to the registered holder of the shares, such as the broker, and the registered holder forwards it to the actual owner.) This annual mailing is called a "proxy statement," and it solicits each shareholder's vote on the directors up for election that year along with various other matters, including shareholder proposals.

The rules regarding shareholder proposals, however, are very complex and often permit the corporation to deny inclusion of a proposal in the proxy statement, meaning the other shareholders are not even told about it. Even if they do include it, and even if the proposal passes, the result is not binding unless the proposal calls for a specific change in the corporation's bylaws (its governing document). In 2018, the five-hundred largest U.S. publicly traded companies (the S&P 500) had fewer than one such proposal per company, and the vast majority of these proposals were defeated.[7] The failure rate is likely to remain high since the institutions that own the vast majority of shares typically focus only on the financial returns of the companies they own.

Shareholder proposals do have the potential to affect corporate behavior. Nevertheless, due to the difficulty of getting them on the ballot and corralling a majority of the shareholders to vote for them, their effect is likely to continue to be quite limited, unless the rules governing them are changed to make this process less difficult. This seems unlikely given that the rules were changed in late 2020 to make submitting shareholder proposals *more* difficult. This leads us to a much larger issue: changing the rules for corporate behavior in general.

Amending the Rules

The key point I want to make about corporate behavior is the same point I made earlier in this book about our economic system. The rules governing corporate behavior, like the rules governing the economy, are the result of the political process, and, therefore, changes to those rules are also a result of that process. The objectivity and fairness of this process is a big issue given the outsize influence corporations have on it.

This influence has soared in the past several years due to the Supreme Court's 2010 ruling in *Citizens United v. Federal Election Commission*, which extended the protections of the First Amendment's free speech clause to corporations. Specifically, the case permitted corporations to spend unlimited amounts of money advocating for the election or defeat of individual candidates for public office. The Court stated that if an individual has free speech rights and can spend whatever they want to influence an election, associations of individuals should also have those rights.

That may sound logical on the surface, but dig one inch and a huge problem becomes evident. When an individual speaks, they have control of what they say. When an association of individuals speak, such as a corporation with hundreds of thousands of shareholders, the vast majority of the individuals have no control or even awareness of what is being said. The one who decides the corporation's positions on issues, the CEO, can amplify his or her own voice by using the resources that belong to the shareholders without their consent or knowledge.

The case essentially turned a process in which lobbyists had significant sway over elected officials into one in which lobbyists can almost control elected officials. If an official does not come around to supporting the view of the corporation's lobbyist, the corporation can simply spend whatever it takes to replace them with an official who would.

To say *Citizens United* further shifted the balance of power in favor of corporations would be an understatement. Robert Reich, who served as secretary of labor in the Clinton administration and is a professor at the University of California, Berkeley, has documented how corporations make a much better return on investments in the political process than they do on investments in anything else, including their own businesses. Corporations can spend millions of dollars on the political process and expect to receive benefits worth many times what they spend in more permissive regulations, tax breaks, and outright subsidies.

If the actions of a corporation didn't have any effect on the world outside the corporation, this spending would be less of a problem. In such a world, the corporation would merely be persuading (or, in the post–*Citizens United* world, coercing) officials to enact policies to benefit the corporation and its shareholders without impacting others. That world may exist in someone's theoretical model, but it couldn't be further from reality.

Virtually every action in the business world has some effect, intended or unintended, on others. Some of these effects are obvious, such as the pollution caused by a company's failure to install proper equipment, the community services cut by a local government so that it can afford to provide corporate subsidies, the demise of small companies when special tax incentives are lavished by the government on large ones, and the jobs lost when a company decides to replace employees with machines or cheaper employees elsewhere. Economists call these costs imposed on others "negative externalities." They occur when a company's activities impose a cost on a party "external" to the company. Therefore, the company has little incentive to cut back on such activities.

Many externalities, like pollution, are easy to measure, but many others are subtle or harder to quantify. When Facebook's algorithm provides users with increasingly provocative links about politics and the state of the world to get their attention, our nation suffers increasing anger and polarization. When Amazon's efficient means of distribution puts local retailers out of business, communities suffer in all sorts of ways, from depressed local economies to less vibrant, welcoming, and safe streets. When a ride-sharing app makes using a private vehicle easier than taking public transportation, traffic increases and mass transit deteriorates. When many companies commit countless daily acts that affect the environment, some only in tiny ways, the cumulative effect on our climate over time may prove catastrophic. Direct and clear harm caused by businesses is bad, but at least we have the potential to identify and address it. Indirect and subtle harm, like environmental impacts, can easily be missed. Even when it's identified, its causes and the means for addressing it may not be as clear.

The only way the cost of these activities on others can be mitigated is through government action. One way that works for some of these activities is to make the company "internalize" the cost of the harm they impose on others. Specifically, the government's economists can estimate in dollars the amount of harm certain activities cause and then impose a tax or fee on the company for that amount. If the fee is significant, the activity will be curtailed. If the activity is not sufficiently curtailed, the fee can be increased until it is.

On the other hand, if the activity is important enough to the company, they will pay the fee and the activity will continue. But at least in that case, society will be reimbursed for the harm done *and* the company will take the harm into account in making future decisions. For example, the government could require auto makers to pay a fee related to how much pollution their vehicles emit and the cost to society of that pollution. Such a sliding fee would reduce sales of the most polluting vehicles. The money collected by the government from its fees on the remaining sales could be used to promote mass transit and other more environmentally friendly forms of transit, undoing some of the harm that those vehicles cause.

Any such remedy for the harm done by corporations, however, can only be implemented by government officials—the same government officials who are often biased toward large, wealthy corporate interests that provide much of the funding for their campaigns and support for their careers. Reducing such influence by overturning *Citizens United* and restricting the flow of cash would require three-quarters of the states to agree to an amendment to the U.S. Constitution—something very unlikely to happen in the current political environment. Getting the Supreme Court to revisit and overturn the case seems equally unlikely since the case was decided just one decade ago and justices serve for life. Therefore, in the foreseeable future, change will happen only if we focus on our own role in this process as citizens.

Some view citizens as customers to be served, such as Jared Kushner, President Trump's son-in-law, who stated that the government should "achieve successes and efficiencies for our customers."[8] Others view citizens as dependents, such as Kushner's father-in-law when he talked about stripping certain Americans of their citizenship. We are neither the government's customers nor its dependents—we are its bosses. If elected officials ignore the common good for the good of those who fund their campaigns, the answer is not to ask them to ignore their donors. The answer is to fire them by voting them out of office.

Inspiring people to take a greater interest in the issues that impact their lives, see past the incessant rhetoric to identify good policies, and support those politicians who champion them is not easy. Nevertheless, there is simply no other practical way to effect change in our nation. I like to think that this book will have some role in that process.

Countless movements that successfully rile people up but fail to achieve any real change show just how difficult it is to impact public policy. In many cases, such efforts achieve symbolic victories, which some people mistake for real change. This leads them to think that the battle has been won and real victory achieved, diverting them from further action. The "Statement of the Purpose of a Corporation" issued in 2019 by the Business Roundtable and signed by almost two hundred CEOs of America's largest corporations is an example of this. Under pressure due to the widening economic divide in our nation, these CEOs declared that "companies should not only serve their shareholders, but also deliver value to their customers, invest in employees, deal fairly with suppliers and support the communities in which they operate."[9] This is a nice statement and it remains just that—a nice statement devoid of any indication of how or when it will result in any change in the real world.

Another example is the Occupy Wall Street movement, which successfully raised awareness of growing economic inequality. When people mention the "1 percent" or the "99 percent," we all know what they're talking about largely because of this movement. Nevertheless, the protestors who occupied parks in major cities failed to occupy, or have any real presence in, the places where policies are actually made—legislatures and government bureaucracies. Believing in or talking about good policies alone does not necessarily change anything, no matter how much people may think it should or hope it would. Since Occupy Wall Street appeared on the scene in 2011, the gap between the 1 percent and everyone else has grown even faster, proving that point.

On the other hand, the Tea Party movement, which called for lower taxes and less government spending in the wake of the Great Recession, may have been wrong on the economics (there is a lot more on that in our discussion of the economic cycle in part 4), but they were exactly right on the politics. In the 2010 midterm elections, the *New York Times* identified 138 candidates for Congress with significant Tea Party support, approximately a third of whom were elected to office.[10] Their presence in Congress may be one of the reasons the government's response to the Great Recession was not as robust as most economists think it should have been, resulting in a slower recovery.

How to go about organizing is beyond the scope of this book. Nevertheless, I hope this book helps with what may be the most difficult part of bringing about change—identifying ideas that will work in the real world, marshalling the arguments in favor of them, and motivating others to support them and the politicians who are committed to implementing them. The better the ideas and the clearer the arguments, the easier the mobilizing. As the preface to this book said, "Democracy is not a spectator sport." Shakespeare, not surprisingly, said it much more artfully in a different context when he said, "The fault, dear Brutus, is not in our stars, but in ourselves."

Before we get to our democratic rights and the role of our government in the economy, we need to discuss a particular emerging threat to our economy posed by the winner-take-all trend. We are increasingly being put at the mercy of megacompanies with the power to control markets, dictate prices, and set the terms of employment. The next chapter discusses this phenomenon and what we can do about it.

9

BUSINESS CONSOLIDATION AND REDUCED COMPETITION

Why Are More Industries Being Dominated by Fewer Companies?

A monopoly is a terrible thing—until you get one.

—Rupert Murdoch, billionaire
businessman and media tycoon

COST ADVANTAGES AND NETWORK EFFECTS

As we discussed in chapter 2, the Technological Revolution has greatly reduced, if not eliminated, the cost of doing business on a mass scale, giving unprecedented advantages to the biggest producers. These economies of scale make it difficult to compete with them, causing more industries to be dominated by one company (a "monopoly") or a small group of companies (an "oligopoly"). This phenomenon has allowed retail to be done on a previously unimaginably large scale by Amazon, transportation services to be offered almost ubiquitously by Uber, and almost every conceivable kind of video entertainment to be offered when and where it's wanted by Netflix.

The increased advantage for megabusinesses spans most industries. One academic study found that more than three-fourths of U.S. industries have experienced an increase in concentration levels over the period from 1996 to 2016 and firms in industries with the largest increases in concentration "have enjoyed higher profit margins, positive abnormal stock returns, and more profitable [merger and acquisition] deals, suggesting that market power is becoming an important source of value."[1] A study by Barclays noted that since 2000, business concentration has increased more than 60 percent.[2]

Big companies have almost always had an advantage. What has changed in the last couple of decades is that competing with Amazon, Uber, Netflix, and many other major businesses has become almost impossible given their ability to spread their fixed costs among the massive number of customers the global internet has provided to them. The competitive advantage their size provides also gives them the ability to negotiate rock-bottom prices for the goods and services they need to run their businesses as well as more leverage in dealing with labor—in other words, even more economies of scale.

Many of these huge new companies benefit from more than just cost advantages. They benefit from a phenomenon known as a "network effect." When you buy bread from a bakery, you really don't care how many other people shop there. Your main concerns are the quality and price of the bread you're buying. However, when you choose a social-networking site or which software to buy, you care a great deal about how many others are choosing that site or that software because their choice affects the benefit you get. How?

A social-networking site such as Facebook has almost 3 billion users and you're likely to find more friends, family, and acquaintances among them than you are among the vastly smaller number of users on some other site. This is true even if the other site is better designed and simpler to use—your primary interest is connecting with other people, and they're on Facebook.

Similarly, if every computer you ever used had Microsoft software, you'll probably be more interested in buying Microsoft software when you buy a new computer. This is not because Microsoft software is inherently better. It's simply because you would have to spend time and effort learning new programs, or because using a different program from the one that you use at work might make it hard to transfer your files, or because most (almost all?) of the files you need to access use Microsoft software. With network effects, the more other people choose to use the good or service, the greater the benefit to you and the more likely other people will choose it as well.

Technology and network effects have reduced competition and enabled a smaller number of larger firms to control more and more sectors of the economy. Why is this a problem? When an industry has many competitors, each company feels pressure to keep prices low, develop innovative products, and provide good customer service in order not to lose business. The less competition a company faces, the less it feels these pressures. For example, to get a sense of the "customer service" many of these dominant companies feel they need to provide, try negotiating a change to the multipage, miniscule-font "terms of service" most of them require you to explicitly accept before they will do any business with you.

Bigger, more dominant companies also have greater leverage when dealing with workers, more ability to finance and implement labor-saving technology, and extra influence with politicians when they seek tax reductions, regulatory rollbacks, and other benefits from the government. All of this clout with consumers, suppliers, workers, and the government also allows these companies to grab a larger share of the economic pie for their owners—furthering the shift of income from labor to capital. As the venture capitalist Peter Thiel said, "Competition is for losers."

PROMOTING COMPETITION

What can be done to promote competition and prevent power from being consolidated? The first step is to recognize that many of the government's own laws and policies create or exacerbate these trends.

A few of these laws intentionally and explicitly set up monopolies in order to prevent competition. For example, the government grants patents on products, such as pharmaceuticals, which give the owner of the patent a monopoly on selling that product. It grants copyrights on intellectual property, such as computer software, which give the owner a monopoly on licensing that product for others to use or enjoy. The justification for these monopolies is that we would have many fewer new inventions or products if developers were not granted a period of time where they would be the exclusive seller of what they developed. That's the only way they can be guaranteed a return on the huge amount of time and money needed to invent and create new things.

Nevertheless, with regard to certain types of new products, particularly important new drugs, some restrictions on pricing seem reasonable. Patents should incent companies to develop new drugs by allowing them to charge prices that enable them to recoup the significant development costs and earn decent profits. Patents should not allow prices that enable them to earn outsize profits by taking advantage of people's medical needs.

Unlike laws that intentionally create monopolies in order to encourage innovation, many laws that tilt the playing field in favor of larger, richer companies have little justification. Hypercomplex regulations, excessive licensing requirements, and convoluted tax laws that are routinely addressed by a large company's legal department can put a smaller company with a small or, in many cases, nonexistent legal department at a significant disadvantage.

Furthermore, our legal system gives large companies with deep pockets the ability to flood not only their competitors, but also anyone potentially standing in their way, with costly litigation. The

"American Rule" regarding legal fees provides that, in general, each party in a court case pays their own legal fees. Therefore, lawsuits are a particularly useful tactic for large companies that can access staff lawyers to sue smaller companies that often need to hire expensive outside law firms to defend them. Even if the party being sued gets the case against them dismissed or ultimately wins the case, they're still stuck with the legal expense of establishing they did nothing wrong. I once overheard someone asking a staff lawyer for a large company that was particularly aggressive in suing its competitors whether their job was stressful. The lawyer responded by saying, "I don't get stress. I give stress."

Clearly, many elected representatives give lip service to the virtues of small business and often affectionately refer to them as "mom and pops." Additionally, the federal government's Small Business Administration "provides counseling, capital, and contracting expertise as the nation's only go-to resource and voice for small businesses."[3] Most local governments have a similar division that aims to help small business. Nevertheless, many of the laws and regulations that, in many cases unintentionally, advantage larger companies remain in place and seem to grow in number and complexity over time.

Increasing economies of scale and network effects are posing a serious and unprecedented threat to robust competition. These are formidable forces, so undoing government policies that advantage big businesses will just slow down the problem. In the past, the government has tried three main approaches to reining in companies that start to dominate or monopolize an industry.

The first involves either breaking up companies if they become too big and powerful or acting preemptively to stop companies from merging to become so powerful in the first place. The antitrust laws that were adopted over one hundred years ago empower the government to do this. One of the most famous uses of this power occurred in the 1980s when the government broke up the Bell Telephone Company, which had a monopoly on telephones in the United States. The telephone company's monopoly was due to both phenomena discussed above. First, it had great economies of scale, as it was able to spread the fixed costs of its telephone network over millions of users, making it very inexpensive to hook up a new user. Second, it had virtually every person in the United States as a customer, making it difficult, if not impossible, to set up a parallel network. Unlike today's wireless carriers, Bell Telephone was not as welcoming to calls from outside its network.

The government broke the company into several smaller regional telephone companies called "Baby Bells." Since then, there have been mergers among these smaller telephone companies, resulting in two of them, AT&T and Verizon, growing to control approximately 70 percent of the wireless telephone market. Do these two companies wield less market power than the one that controlled essentially 100 percent of the market? Possibly, although there is not much incentive for AT&T and Verizon to compete too hard against each other since the government is unlikely to allow one company to dominate the telephone market.

Economies of scale and network effects are particularly important for many new and important industries, such as those that provide broadband access, social networking, internet search services, and next-day-delivery home shopping. The advantages size and a network offer to the largest companies in these industries don't go away if these companies are simply broken up. As with the telephone industry, these advantages will likely lead to the reemergence of a few dominant companies even after a breakup.

To keep businesses in such an industry numerous and competitive requires a vigilant fight by the government against the tendencies that encourage consolidation. On the other hand, it might also mean giving up some of the benefits of economies of scale and network effects that do flow through to consumers. For example, local phone service became more expensive right after Bell Telephone was broken up because the company used its very profitable long-distance calls to subsidize its local service. Nevertheless, we may not have essentially free long-distance calls and countless other communication innovations today if Bell Telephone had kept its monopoly.

The second approach the government has tried is to simply own and control the business. That's what New York City did in 1940 when it bought the Brooklyn–Manhattan Transit Corporation (the BMT) and the Interborough Rapid Transit Company (the IRT), the two privately owned subway lines operating at the time. It's also why the government runs certain businesses, like the U.S. Postal Service and Amtrak. In mail delivery, rail service, and other businesses that require massive capital investments to operate, size confers critical advantages. Other nations have been even more willing to own businesses that require massive capital investments, like airlines and energy companies. Government-controlled companies are often very much like private monopolies that don't face competition—they tend to not be the most efficient, innovative, or consumer oriented. Take a ride on Amtrak if you want to get a better idea of this problem.

The third approach is to regulate how the business operates and limit what it charges. This is the approach the government has taken with most electric and gas utilities, such as Consolidated Edison, the provider of electricity in New York City. Such regulation can rein in the ability of a dominant business to overcharge consumers and strong-arm employees. Regulation's ability to incentivize companies to better serve their customers and come up with imaginative new products that benefit their customers is, however, more limited.

As we have already discussed, corporate heavyweights that come to dominate an industry are able to grab a larger share of the economic pie for their investors, reducing the share for labor. Some economic problems have relatively easy answers. This one doesn't. I called breaking up companies, public ownership, and regulation three "approaches" to this problem rather than "solutions" for a reason.

Each industry is different, and power is concentrated for different reasons. It could be economies of scale (as in the case of electric utilities), a network effect (as in the case of Facebook), a hyperaggressive approach to any competition (as in the case of Rockefeller's near monopoly on oil refining in the early 1900s), or any combination of these. The effect of that power once gained may be benign (such as when we get access to a vast database of job opportunities) or ruinous (such as when one company curates all the news we see). Any response to such concentration of power must consider these differences. It needs to weigh the benefits that large organizations can offer, in potentially lower prices due to the economies of scale or a more robust network for users, against the costs that their power and influence can impose on workers and society in general.

This type of "cost-benefit analysis" is very popular among economists and justifiably so. It weighs the strengths (benefits) of each alternative—such as letting a large organization dominate the market, breaking it up, taking it over, or regulating it—against the weaknesses (costs) of such alternative. Whichever alternative has the greatest benefits compared to the costs is the one to choose. The trick is to include all the costs and benefits regardless of how difficult they are to calculate or put a dollar value on and who bears them. This trick is often hard to pull off with regard to the costs of concentrated power, which can include innovations or inventions we may never see, less diversity in product types, disillusionment on the part of potential competitors, and, in general, a less dynamic and competitive economy.

The trend of increasing power, wealth, and influence in larger and more dominant businesses will not stop by itself. Like climate change, it happens gradually and almost imperceptibly. Also, like climate change, we ignore it at our peril.

The need for collective action to address significant economic problems head-on rather than ignore them is a lesson our nation learned in connection with downturns in the economy. Since the Great Depression, people have come to expect the government to help pull the economy out of recessions and mitigate swings in the economic cycle. What tools the government uses to do this is the subject of the next part of this book.

Part IV

THE ECONOMIC CYCLE

10

BOOM AND BUST

Must What Goes Up Come Down?

A recession is when your neighbor loses his job. A depression is when you lose yours. And recovery is when Jimmy Carter loses his.

—Ronald Reagan during the 1980 presidential campaign

WHAT IS A RECESSION?

The coronavirus-related recession and the Great Recession of 2008 are the two most recent downturns in the economy. There have been, by many counts, at least twelve other recessions since the Great Depression in the early 1930s. What exactly are these downturns in the economy, and why do they keep occurring?

Generally, a "recession" is defined as a decline in output (in other words, the GDP) for two consecutive calendar quarters. So, if output drops from the last calendar quarter and this happens again in the next calendar quarter, the economy is usually viewed as being in a recession. The term "depression" doesn't have a

widely accepted definition like the term "recession," but it generally refers to a particularly severe recession. How severe? In the
last hundred years, only the "Great Depression" that occurred in
the 1930s is consistently referred to as a depression. The recession
that occurred in 2008 is generally called the "Great Recession"
because it was worse than most recessions, but not as bad as the
Great Depression.

Since most of us don't follow the quarterly GDP numbers, how
would we know the economy is in a recession? As we discussed
in chapter 4, the economy's total output of goods and services
equals total spending equals total incomes. Therefore, if output
drops, spending and incomes drop as well. This means we would
see greater unemployment (because fewer workers are needed
to produce less output), falling incomes (as more workers are
laid off), mostly falling prices (as businesses compete to sell to a
smaller and less well-off number of customers), and more bank-
ruptcies, foreclosures, and evictions.

So, what happens when incomes drop? People spend even less.
And what happens when people spend even less? Incomes drop
even more. And what happens when incomes drop even more?
I think you get the picture: the economy enters a downward spiral. This raises the question: How does this downward spiral get
started in the first place?

WHAT CAUSES A RECESSION?

Demand Shocks

The fact that the economic term for a severe downturn is the
same as the psychological term for a severe downturn—a "depression"—provides a clue as to its cause.* What changes in a typical

---

* I am using the psychological term "depression" informally and not to refer
to any specific clinical set of symptoms that could be triggered by a chemical
imbalance or physiological problem.

depression (or, more generally, in a recession) is the overall mood and outlook in a society. An infectious gloom takes over, people spend less, output decreases, and incomes drop. This change in outlook is called a "demand shock" because people's willingness to spend abruptly declines and they "demand" fewer goods and services.

A demand shock is a psychological phenomenon on a mass scale. When the economy turns down, factories don't crumble, workers don't forget their skills, and the economy's resources don't disappear. You can test the industrial capacity of factories, the productive potential of businesses, and the skill level of workers right before a typical recession begins and right after it has begun and you will not see any difference. What changes is people's outlook. Although a recession may start as a purely psychological phenomenon, it very quickly has real-world consequences.

Why do people suddenly change their outlook, become pessimistic, and start the vicious cycle of less spending and lower incomes? Economists and businesspeople often point to an abrupt crash in the value of stocks, real estate, or some other asset that has grown rapidly in value as the cause of the gloom. This phenomenon is called an asset "bubble" and the crash in price is referred to as the "bursting" of the bubble. When that asset affects many people, like stocks in 1929 or housing in 2008, the bursting of the bubble is likely to cause a demand shock and an economic downturn in its wake. This raises the question of why bubbles form in the first place. Why do the returns on some assets take off only to crash and burn later?

The answer (yet again) is mass psychology. During good times, when the GDP is growing, people get optimistic. They invest in stocks, real estate, businesses, and other assets with the expectation that they will earn great returns. On many occasions, an asset with particularly high returns attracts unusual attention. It draws in a large number of investors, causing its price to soar even more, well in excess of anything rational analysis would predict or justify. John Maynard Keynes referred to this phenomenon as "the result of animal spirits—a spontaneous urge to action rather than inaction, and not as the outcome of a weighted average of quantitative benefits multiplied by quantitative probabilities."[1]

Many investors who get caught up in an asset bubble realize that the price they are paying and any loans they may be taking to buy the rising asset may be foolish. Nevertheless, they assume there will always be an even greater fool to whom they'll be able to sell their investment at a profit. Herd mentality, a constant drumbeat of anecdotes about how other investors are getting rich, and a fear of missing out can cause a lot of people to act foolishly. Economists call this the "greater fool theory," and it works until there are no more fools left and the investor I would call the "greatest fool" gets stuck with the asset when the bubble finally bursts.

Let's look at the Great Recession of 2008 to learn more about this phenomenon. In the early 2000s when the economy was strong, lenders got caught up in the optimism about the housing market. They became more liberal in qualifying people for mortgage loans. Many even started providing mortgage loans to people with questionable (or actually bad) credit to enable them to buy homes they probably couldn't afford. More money for mortgage loans led to more home buying that led to rising home prices. This attracted the attention of investors who started buying homes to flip (resell quickly) or to rent to tenants (and collect what the investors thought would be ever-increasing rents). As home prices escalated, lenders lowered their standards even further with some lenders making what those in the industry called "NINJA" loans: loans to people with no income, no job, and no assets.

What were the lenders funding this buying spree and boom in housing prices thinking? Many believed that they could earn a quick profit by selling these loans to other investors, so they no longer had to care whether the loan was repaid. And mostly, they were correct. Nevertheless, no matter how many times ownership of these loans changed hands, each loan had an ultimate buyer willing to finance it. So, what were *they* thinking?

To the extent the final buyers of these loans were actually thinking about what they were doing instead of just being caught up in
the speculative frenzy, they correctly thought one of two things
would happen: The borrower would make the payments on the
mortgage loan *or* the borrower would not make the payments.
If the borrower made the payments, the buyer of the loan would
earn more money than they could by buying loans made to creditworthy borrowers, since riskier loans have higher interest rates.
If the borrower failed to make the payments, they would simply
take back the home (in other words, foreclose on it) and sell it for
a profit into a market of forever-increasing real estate prices. They
figured either way, they won. Yes, even sophisticated investors
with prestigious degrees, fancy spreadsheets, and huge incomes
can fall prey to infectious optimism and forget what we all know—
the price of any major asset cannot continuously soar forever. That
sounds right, but why is it right?

In the decade before the Great Recession (1996 to 2006), housing prices went up a total of approximately 93 percent.[2] Median
incomes over that period, however, increased a total of approximately 36 percent.[3] A situation where the cost of housing eats
up a larger and larger share of each household's total budget will
cause fewer and fewer Americans to be able to afford a home.[†]
This situation has to come to an end at some point. That point
was 2007, when home price increases slowed and turned negative
later in the year.

The question remains: Why do bubbles burst abruptly rather
than slowly deflate back to a more sustainable growth level and
thereby create less of a "shock" to demand? The answer, again,
can be found in human nature.

Each investor drawn to the housing market in the mid-2000s
expected great returns and, for many years, those expectations

---

† Housing values in specific markets, such as Manhattan or San Francisco,
can grow faster than the economy as a whole since these values rely on the
spending of a relatively small group of people whose incomes are growing faster
than the economy.

were met. However, as homes became increasingly unaffordable in 2007 and price increases slowed down, new investors started to look elsewhere to invest. Additionally, many existing investors started to put their homes on the market in order to cash out at what was beginning to look like the market peak or to simply get rid of an asset that was beginning to lose its luster. The decrease in buyers and increase in sellers led housing price increases to slow even further. In turn, an even greater number of real estate investors looked to sell and lock in their profits (or avoid future losses). The downward spiral was set off as investors started seeing prices fall, ran for the exits, flooded the market, and burst the bubble. The stagnating home prices of 2007 were followed by two years in which prices dropped by over 6 percent on average each year.[4]

The market crash was accelerated by the extensive use of "leverage" (yet another synonym for debt) to buy real estate. Why? Because if I used $500,000 of my own money to buy a house and its value plummets to $350,000, I still have a $350,000 interest in that house. If I choose to keep the house, every dollar that the house goes up in value from that low point is a dollar in my pocket. If I choose to sell the house, I lock in a $150,000 loss.

On the other hand, if I used $100,000 of my own money and a $400,000 mortgage loan to buy the house, my interest in the house (my full $100,000 investment) is totally wiped out. Furthermore, even if the house goes up in value, not one dollar of the first $50,000 increase will go into my pocket because the loan will still exceed the value of the house. Probably more importantly, I will have to make monthly payments on the $400,000 mortgage loan for a house that is now worth only $350,000. In essence, I can increase my net wealth by $50,000 simply by abandoning the house—I lose a house worth $350,000 but get relieved of a $400,000 debt.[‡] It's no wonder so many of the riskier mortgage

---

‡ Most mortgage loans made in connection with the purchase of a home are non-recourse, which means the lender can acquire the home in the event of default but cannot acquire anything else—they cannot take any of the borrower's other assets or income. The lender would, however, report the default to a

loans made in the years before the Great Recession went bad when the market started to turn down.

While we might find it easy to understand this phenomenon of a bursting bubble, the event's timing remains a mystery. Investors could make a lot of money by riding an asset bubble up and selling just before it bursts. All sorts of indicators, from stock prices dropping to interest rates on short-term bonds exceeding those on long-term bonds (the much-cited "inverted yield curve"), are discussed as possible clues as to when the economy is on the verge of a recession. As Paul Samuelson, the author of an introductory economics textbook used by generations of college students, quipped, the stock market has predicted nine out of the last five recessions. Economists have not had much success in predicting the future of the economy either. Like psychologists and, for that matter, everyone else, they have a hard time foreseeing the precise time when the national mood will change.

That said, a few people have had success in making such predictions. Legend has it that Joseph Kennedy, President Kennedy's father, decided to sell stocks right before they crashed in 1929 after a shoeshine boy gave him a stock tip. He thought that if even shoeshine boys were buying and selling stocks, the stock market was bid up as far as it could go—every spare dollar was already invested in the market, so the only direction the market could go was down. More recently, hedge-fund manager Michael Burry used derivative securities (specifically, credit default swaps) to bet that housing prices would plummet. He endured skepticism for years from his funders as they regularly lost money on his bets. As depicted in both the book and the film *The Big Short*, he managed to hang on until the housing bubble eventually burst and he could collect enormous winnings. Nevertheless, what was great for Joseph Kennedy and Michael Burry was very bad for the economy.

---

credit-reporting agency, which could result in harm to a defaulting borrower if they were to seek a new loan.

Supply Shocks

Occasionally, something other than a demand shock sets off a downturn. A recession can also be set off by direct physical harm to a nation, which reduces its ability to produce goods and services. If a significant number of people cannot work or are killed (due to a war or a pandemic, for example) or if a significant part of the physical infrastructure or supplies needed for production are destroyed or not readily available (due to something like a natural catastrophe or hostile action), production will decline. Economists call events like these, which directly impact the supply of goods and services and can cause particularly troublesome downturns in the economy, "supply shocks."

Prior to 2020, the classic example of a supply shock recession was the one that followed the oil embargo imposed by the members of the Organization of the Petroleum Exporting Countries (OPEC). The embargo targeted the United States and other nations OPEC perceived as supporting Israel during its 1973 Yom Kippur War. Since oil is essential to virtually all productive activities (even writers need electricity for their computers), the decrease in the supply of oil and increase in its price made almost all types of production much more expensive and difficult. A severe economic downturn predictably followed.

Much more recently, we have unfortunately had another example of a recession caused by a supply shock. The coronavirus caused the government to shut down whole sectors of the economy, thereby suddenly reducing the supply of many goods and services. If the government didn't shut down so much of the economy, there would have been an even greater death toll, presumably accompanied by major absences from work by frightened employees, thereby potentially reducing output even more. However the nation responded, the coronavirus was destined to interfere with the economy and cause less stuff to be produced, less stuff to be bought, and less money to be earned. As you may expect, a supply shock also depresses consumer sentiment, usually creating a demand shock in its wake.

You can look at the causes of a slump in the economy the way you look at the causes of a slump for a person. A person suffering from a psychological malaise is similar to an economy suffering from a demand shock. A gloomy and depressed outlook overcomes them both, rendering them less productive. A person suffering from a severe physical ailment, like a broken leg or an obstructed artery, is like an economy suffering from a supply shock. A direct impairment to their body renders them less productive. The person suffering from the physical ailment is likely to get demoralized as well, just as a supply shock is likely to cause its own demand shock, potentially making the return to productivity more challenging.

Now that we have discussed what causes economic downturns, we can turn to the question of what the government should do about them. In chapters 11 and 12, we'll discuss the Federal Reserve System and one of the two main tools used to fight a downturn: monetary policy. In chapter 13, we'll discuss the other main tool: fiscal policy (government spending and tax policy).

THE FEDERAL RESERVE SYSTEM AND BANKING

What Is the Fed's Role, and How Is New Money Created?

It is well that the people of the nation do not understand our banking and monetary system, for if they did, I believe there would be a revolution before tomorrow morning.

—Henry Ford

WHAT IS THE FED, AND WHAT DOES IT DO?

The Federal Reserve System of the United States, almost always referred to as the "Fed," is America's central bank. All but the smallest nations have a central bank. Although their names, like the Bank of England, the Reserve Bank of Australia, and the Swiss National Bank, are different from the Fed's, they are all responsible for conducting their nation's monetary policy—controlling their nation's money supply, and, thereby, influencing interest rates and economic activity. The countries that use the euro are the big exception—they have one common central bank, the European Central Bank.

The Fed was set up by the U.S. government as an independent agency in 1913. It is headquartered in Washington, D.C., with twelve regional reserve banks located in major cities throughout the United States that are responsible for supervising the banks in their jurisdictions. A seven-member board of governors, who are appointed by the president and confirmed by the Senate for fourteen-year terms, oversees the Fed. The president selects one of the seven (again, with the consent of the Senate) to serve as the chair of the Fed for a four-year term. The governors are typically very prominent people from the financial industry and academia. Once appointed, the governors may not be removed from office for their policy views. Their lengthy appointments are intended to help insulate them from day-to-day political pressures. In many ways, the Fed is structured like the U.S. court system: It's separate from the government with officials who serve long terms designed to foster their independence.

The Fed has two main missions. The first is to serve as the bank for banks. People, businesses, government agencies, and, in fact, every public and private organization (except banks) all make deposits at banks. Banks make deposits at the Fed.* Just as you can deposit $100 in a bank, the bank can in turn deposit your $100 into its account at the Fed. Your basic account at your bank is called a checking account; a bank's account at the Fed is called its "reserve account."

Just as you can opt to hold your currency instead of depositing it at the bank, a bank can opt to hold its depositors' money as currency instead of depositing it at the Fed. However, as a practical matter, banks keep the vast majority of their deposits at the Fed and not in their vaults for the same reason people keep most of their money at the bank and not at home—it's easier and safer. Bank "reserves" are simply the bank's deposits at the Fed plus the relatively small amount of currency the bank keeps on hand. The

---

* Under some of the proposals for Central Bank Digital Currencies (mentioned in chapter 3), the Fed would start to offer accounts to everyone.

Fed also oversees the nation's banking system and sets policies to ensure its safety and soundness.

The other main role of the Fed—and the one that's important to our discussion regarding downturns in the economy—is fulfilling its "dual mandate." On one hand, the Fed is charged with promoting maximum employment (which essentially means keeping the economy growing). On the other hand, it's charged with promoting stable prices (which the Fed has interpreted to mean avoiding inflation averaging more than 2 percent per year).

Before the government set up the Fed, the economy was much more volatile. As we have discussed, bank runs and financial "panics" (bank failures, market crashes, economic turbulence, mass layoffs, etc.) were common. At least thirteen separate financial panics occurred in the century before the Fed's creation. While our economy still has its ups and downs, the swings have generally been less extreme since the Fed was set up.

This dual mandate (simultaneously promoting maximum employment and stable prices), however, imposes somewhat contradictory goals. I mentioned in chapter 3 that pumping a lot of new money into the economy would cause people to spend more. Businesses would respond by hiring and producing more, to the extent possible. But if the increase in the amount of money were greater than the increase in output, there would be inflation. On the other hand, putting a lid on new money to prevent inflation would risk not promoting enough spending to maximize employment. The Fed's goal is to find the sweet spot—where it stimulates the economy enough to maximize employment but not enough to stoke inflation.

Before we discuss how increasing the amount of money (something from the financial economy) has such a significant impact on employment and therefore output (the real economy), we need to discuss how new money is created in the first place.

HOW IS MONEY CREATED?

John Kenneth Galbraith, the prolific economist and advisor to several U.S. presidents, once said, "The process by which money is created is so simple that the mind is repelled."[1] His definition of "simple" is a lot different from mine, and I suspect yours as well.

As we discussed, "money" or "the money supply" simply means currency in circulation plus checking account balances. The amount of money, which represents the amount of buying power in the economy, is almost always increasing. For example, in 1960, the money supply was around $140 billion. By January 2022, it had increased almost 150 times to around $20.7 *trillion*.[2] How does this happen, and who got that huge amount of new money?

Congress granted the Fed control over the process by which money is created and prohibited it from creating money and simply handing it to any person, any business, or, in fact, any branch of the government, including Congress or the U.S. Treasury. Therefore, in our current system, when the government wants to spend more money, it cannot just rev up the printing presses to create the additional money. Congress has to raise every single dollar it needs through either taxes or borrowing.

Congress imposed this constraint on itself and delegated the ability to create money to the Fed when it enacted the legislation setting up the Fed. We need to keep in mind that the Fed's control over our money was not something ordained by nature—it was a choice made by Congress over one hundred years ago. Therefore, a future Congress can just as easily remove this constraint, reclaim the power to create money for itself, or set up a new system for creating money.

The reason the U.S. and most governments have constrained themselves in this way and delegated their nation's money-making authority to a central bank is that the absence of such a constraint can be disastrous. Governments given direct access to the money-making machine can lose control of their spending and create so much money that it becomes worthless.

Exactly how does this happen? Rather than raising taxes (which is unpopular, to say the least) or borrowing (which can be difficult or expensive), a nation's government simply creates money to cover the cost of new or growing government programs, especially programs they think will help keep them in power. Creating more money creates inflation, which raises the cost of the programs. So, the government creates even more money to cover the increasingly expensive programs. But then inflation increases even more, so the government has to create an even larger amount of money. This results in a constantly accelerating rate of inflation called "hyperinflation," which ultimately causes the nation's monetary system to crash and burn.

For example, in the 1920s, the Weimar government in Germany created so much new money that people were reported to have burned currency instead of wood to heat their homes and hauled wheelbarrows full of currency to buy a loaf of bread. There are stories of restaurant meals costing more when the bill came than when the food was ordered. Just after World War II, in one of the worst cases of hyperinflation ever, price increases in Hungary reached 41.9 quadrillion percent *per month*, causing the total value of all Hungarian currency in circulation to be worth a fraction of a United States penny.[3] More recently, the government of Zimbabwe was printing 100 trillion–dollar bills (which, as of this writing, sell for about $10 each on eBay) and inflation hit 79.6 billion percent per month. When money loses its value in this way, the range of outcomes varies from a mere economic collapse, as in Zimbabwe, to mass death and a serious threat to world civilization, as in Germany.

When the Fed does exercise its prerogative to create money and increase the money supply, people often say it is "printing" money. I'm all for simplification, but not oversimplification. You probably already know why simply printing currency would not increase the money supply. The newly printed currency would just sit in a locked and guarded government vault and couldn't be spent by anyone (legally). Unless newly printed currency actually gets into the hands of someone who could spend it, the new currency doesn't create buying power for anyone, doesn't impact the economy, and doesn't have any more relevance than a huge pile of green paper. As we discussed, the new currency doesn't even qualify as "money" until it somehow gets into "circulation."

So, how does money get out and about? Through bank lending. When a bank makes a loan, it makes it with brand-new money. Banks don't debit our checking accounts nor do they ask us to hand over some of our own money when they wish to make loans. They simply create the money for loans out of thin air. Whether the borrower takes these newly created dollars in currency (which, if need be, the Fed will supply to the bank to supply to the borrower) or as a credit to their own checking account, the money supply increases by the full amount of this loan. As economists like to say: New money is loaned into existence.

This system where the Fed makes changes in the money supply through banks is called "fractional reserve" banking. Essentially, when you put money in a bank, the bank only retains a "fraction" of that money as a "reserve"—the rest they're allowed to loan out. What fraction of deposits a bank holds as reserves is, as of this writing, up to the bank. Prior to 2020, banks were required to hold at least 10 percent of their total deposits as reserves. So, for example, if you put $1,000 in your checking account, the bank could keep $100 as reserves and lend out the remaining $900. You still have your $1,000 and could spend it whenever you want. But due to the bank's loan to someone, there's now also $900 of brand-new money for the borrower to spend. The money supply has increased by $900. (There was $1,000 before the loan and, through the magic of the banking system, there is $1,900 after the loan.)

At this point you're probably thinking this sounds a lot like what the dishonest bankers did several centuries ago—used people's deposits to make loans for their own private benefit—and you would be mostly right. There are, however, two important improvements that have been made to the banking system.

First, today's bankers are heavily regulated to make sure they are "safe and sound," have sufficient reserves, and use their reserves strictly for the purpose of making loans to others. When a loan is repaid by the borrower, the money goes back into the bank's reserves and is available for new loans and only for new loans. You can think of bank reserves as a pool from which loans are constantly being made, repaid, and made again to every conceivable kind of borrower. If the Fed deems a bank's level of reserves to be inadequate, it can require the bank to increase them or cut back on lending.

Second, unlike the early days of banking, the chances of a bank run today are vastly diminished. When the early bankers faced more withdrawals than they had precious metal left in reserves, the bank failed and the bankers ran for their lives. Today, that cannot happen. Why? FDIC insurance. The Federal Deposit Insurance Corporation, a part of the federal government, insures deposits at U.S. banks up to $250,000 per account. Therefore, in the extremely unlikely event that depositors one day decide to withdraw an amount in excess of the bank's reserves, the bank may fail, but the FDIC will step in and make sure the vast majority of depositors are paid in full. The mere fact that this insurance is in place makes a bank run much less likely. Why race to the branch to withdraw your money when you know you can get your money even if the bank goes bust?[†]

Although this process sounds complicated, it is the process by which all major nations create money. The Nobel Prize–winning economist Milton Friedman famously discussed a much simpler way of increasing the money supply, which he called "helicopter money." Specifically, he wrote about printing currency and then just dropping it from a helicopter. People would pick it up and, thereby, the money supply (currency in circulation) would increase. I assume his example was a metaphor and that he wasn't serious about literally dropping money on people in that way—mailing it to them would be a lot more orderly. Nevertheless, his example does highlight two important points. The first is that there are additional ways to create money other than through

---

† Additionally, the Fed can lend directly to banks in need. This is another protection for depositors since the Fed would clearly do this to avoid a major financial disruption.

bank lending. The second is that money is simply created out of thin air (and in his example, distributed out of thin air as well).

WHO PROFITS FROM CREATING MONEY?

When new currency is printed and dropped from a helicopter or (less chaotically) mailed to individual citizens, it's easy to see who benefits and by how much. When the government simply grabs the currency as it comes off the printing presses and spends it, as the German government did in the 1920s, it's also easy to see where the money goes. What these alternative (and simpler) systems for increasing the money supply have in common is that they involve the government deciding who to enrich with the new money and when—a system that is easily abused, corrupted, and, as discussed, generally not in use today.

So, who is enriched when a bank creates new money to make a loan? Since the borrower has to pay the money back to the bank (with interest), it's not the borrower. They may appreciate and benefit from the loan, but they were not made richer by it. The bank, the other party to this transaction, does benefit. Unfortunately, how they benefit isn't as obvious as in the case of someone picking up cash dropped from a helicopter.

Remember, a bank can only create money to make loans—it cannot create money for any other purpose. The money created by the loan is *not* like a $20 overdraft fee the bank charges you. That fee, like all bank fees, is income for the bank that it can use to pay big bonuses, lobby legislators, or rent excessive amounts of space in major cities. The new money created by the loan goes to the borrower. However, the interest on the loan *is* like the $20 overdraft fee. Whatever the bank earns in interest on loans is income for the bank—it's the benefit to the bank from this money-creation system. At the risk of making a bad pun, this is how banks make money—how they increase the money supply and make a profit for themselves via the interest they charge on loans.

Actually, the bank's benefit from the new money is less than the interest on the loan it made since the bank has to use part of that interest to pay interest on deposits. Nevertheless, as anyone who has ever had an outstanding loan (like credit card debt) and money in a bank at the same time can attest, there's a significant difference between the interest rate charged on a loan and the interest paid on a deposit. That difference, what bankers call "the spread," is an important source of profits for banks. You can think of it as the bank's fee for matching the funds of people who wish to save (the depositors) with people who wish to borrow.

Banks clearly have a key role in our monetary system, so the question remains: Are they doing a good job fulfilling that role? Specifically, how have they used the power to decide who gets a loan, in what amount, and on what terms, as well as the power to decide how much to pay depositors and what fees to charge them? Their decisions can have significant ramifications for fairness, equity, and opportunity.

Generally, the decision makers at banks are not very representative of society, either from a gender and racial perspective or from an income and economic perspective (the latter due to the well-above-average salaries paid to such people). They may make assumptions about the creditworthiness of particular groups or the desirability of attracting depositors and making loans in certain areas.

For example, urban areas with primarily ethnic and racial minorities were "redlined" for many years, preventing people in those neighborhoods from obtaining most real estate loans. Although this practice was outlawed in the 1960s, the effects of underinvestment in those communities caused decay and urban blight. It also prevented many marginalized people from building equity through the post–World War II boom in housing values. These effects, and the great wealth gap to which they contributed, are readily apparent today.

Would broadening the bank's customer base harm profits? Given the demographics of the industry, that question is unlikely to be answered by the banking industry itself. Nevertheless, since banks are licensed by the government, the government could insist on a broader and more inclusive mandate as a condition for the license. In the event that it does, we would see the effect more robust banking services have on underserved populations and the effect those additional services have on bank profits. We (including the bankers among us) might be pleasantly surprised.

Finally, whether you feel well served by the banking system or not, you may be wondering what effect, if any, this system of money creation through bank lending has on you and the economy in general. How this system impacts our lives and our ability to address downturns in the economy is the subject of the next chapter.

For now, you may simply find it comforting to know that there is a somewhat independent institution, the Fed, in charge of regulating the money supply and that "greedy bankers" or government officials cannot just create new money and pocket it. Whatever your comfort level is at this point, however, it may change after we discuss exactly how the Fed controls the amount of money in the next section, and then how it affects our economy.

HOW DOES THE FED CHANGE THE AMOUNT OF MONEY?

Banks are eager to lend money since the interest they earn on loans enables them to pay the interest they owe to their depositors and make profits for themselves. The Fed has tools to influence exactly how eager banks are to lend and, therefore, to influence the amount of new money being created.

The Fed added a new tool for influencing lending and money creation in late 2008—it started paying a small amount of interest on bank reserve accounts. Banks had previously not earned interest on the reserves they held at the Fed. The idea is that the more interest banks receive on their reserves, the less incentive they have to withdraw those reserves to make loans. Similarly, if a bank earns less or no interest on its reserves, it has a greater incentive to withdraw them to make loans. The Fed has the ability to set this interest rate, which, as of this writing, is just 0.15 percent. Think about how your own willingness to leave money in your bank account can be influenced by how much interest your bank pays and you will understand how the Fed uses this tool to influence the willingness of banks to use their reserves to make loans.

The Fed's longstanding and customary method for influencing lending, however, is by directly changing the amount of bank reserves. The idea is that an increase in the amount of bank reserves is likely to increase lending and money creation. Similarly, a decrease in the amount of bank reserves is likely to decrease lending and money creation. How would the Fed increase the amount of a bank's reserves? By buying debt from the bank. An example will show how this works.

Suppose Citibank has loaned out most or all of its reserves. What does Citibank have to show for all of the loans it made? A stack of debt from its borrowers—the people, businesses, and governments who borrowed from Citibank. Now, let's suppose the Fed bought $5 billion of this debt from Citibank. It would credit Citibank's reserve account with the $5 billion purchase price. Citibank would now have $5 billion more in reserves and, therefore, a greater interest in making as well as ability to make new loans and, thereby, create new money.

Where did the Fed get the $5 billion to buy the debt? It simply made it up. (Remember, we are all spending fiat money now—money simply made up by the government, specifically by its central bank with the assistance of private banks, like Citibank.) The Fed took the $5 billion of debt from Citibank and "paid" for it by simply increasing the balance of Citibank's reserve account on its computers by $5 billion.

"Open market operations" is the name for the specific process by which the Fed buys (and sells) debt from banks because it does this in the same "open market" that other institutions buy and sell debt. These operations are conducted, not at the Fed's headquarters in Washington, D.C., but in America's financial capital, New

York City. The Federal Reserve Bank of New York, one of the twelve regional reserve banks, conducts these operations from its Renaissance palace–inspired headquarters in lower Manhattan (which you can and definitely should visit and join one of their many scheduled tours).

The specific debt the Fed buys is generally U.S. government bonds, and it buys them in the same way any buyer of government bonds would: It tries to buy them at the lowest possible price that would get the bank to sell. The Fed has bought trillions of dollars of bonds this way, and as of December 2021 held over $8 trillion worth of them.[4] The interest the Fed receives on the bonds they own funds their operations. Any amount in excess of their expenses is forwarded to the U.S. Treasury and is used by our government in the same way it uses the money it receives from taxes. In 2020, the Fed remitted $88.5 billion to the government in this fashion.[5]

If the Fed is on a bond-buying spree (as it was, big-time, after the Great Recession in 2008 and again after the coronavirus hit in March 2020),[‡] bank reserves will grow significantly. As reserves grow, banks become more interested in making new loans. Why? Because, as we discussed, by making loans, banks make a profit on the interest they earn. But banks need to do something to get more people to borrow: They need to lower the interest rates they charge on loans.

The interest rate is the cost of a loan the way the airfare is the cost of a plane trip. If the government suddenly handed each airline a bunch of new planes, the airlines would need to lower airfares to get more people to fly. That's the only way the airlines could attract additional passengers, fill up the new planes, and make a profit from them. Similarly, when the Fed increases bank reserves, the banks have to lower interest rates to get more people to borrow.

---

‡ The Fed typically purchases bonds issued by the U.S. Treasury with maturities of less than five years through its open-market operations. After the Great Recession, it engaged in "quantitative easing," which meant that it started buying a much broader spectrum of bonds, including bonds issued by other entities and with longer durations.

The Fed can also *decrease* bank reserves by reversing the process described above. The Fed can sell bonds to banks and deduct the price of the bonds from the bank's reserve account. The reserves deducted from a bank's reserve account by the Fed simply disappear. Lower bank reserves reduce a bank's ability to make loans. Rather than tell the customers who apply for loans late in the day that they have run out of the reserves needed to make loans, banks simply raise interest rates, reducing the demand for loans to an amount that they can accommodate. Therefore, interest rates go up, fewer loans are made, and less money is created. As a practical matter, the way the Fed usually reduces the money supply is by simply letting bonds in its portfolio mature (in other words, letting the principal amount owed under the bond come due). It then accepts the principal amount back from the bond issuer and makes that repayment disappear.

This is how the Fed changes the money supply and thereby "sets" interest rates. It doesn't set interest rates the way the government sets tax rates. Rather, interest rates are determined by the market, the way the price of most things are determined. If lenders outnumber borrowers, interest rates drop, and if borrowers outnumber lenders, interest rates go up.

Specifically, the Fed has a target range (typically a 0.25 percent range) for one particularly important interest rate—the "federal funds rate." (The target range for the federal funds rate, as of this writing in early 2022, is at a historical low of 0 to 0.25 percent, although the Fed announced that it planned to increase the rate several times later in 2022.) If the federal funds rate is outside this range, the Fed can nudge it into the range by buying or selling bonds to banks through its open-market operations. As we discussed, the Fed could also change the rate of interest it pays on bank reserve accounts and, thereby, affect bank lending and the federal funds rate.

What is the federal funds rate? It's the interest rate banks charge each other for overnight loans. For example, a bank might commit to too much lending. It could then borrow reserves from another bank and would pay an interest rate equal to the federal funds rate for that loan.

This obscure-sounding interest rate may seem irrelevant to most people. Nevertheless, it influences every other interest rate, from the rate on your home mortgage loan, to the rate on your credit card balance, to the rate you would pay if you needed a loan to start a business. The federal funds rate is the interest rate on a loan with essentially no risk (such as an overnight loan to a bank). Therefore, it sets a floor for the interest rate on all other loans. How much higher the interest rate on any other loan will be depends on the creditworthiness of the borrower, how long the money will be tied up, the purpose of the loan, and many other factors.

You can think of the interest rate on any particular loan like the premium for insurance on any particular car. The insurer has a base price for a perfect driver in some perfect neighborhood with a perfect car. A real person in the real world is going to have a higher insurance premium. They will pay that base price increased for all sorts of reasons, such as a bad driving record, previous insurance claims, living in a high crime area, or having a sports car.

With regard to a loan, that base price is the federal funds rate. The actual interest rate on any loan is that base rate increased to compensate the lender for the risk associated with the particular borrower and the particular loan. Sometimes, the additional risk is small and the interest rate on the loan is close to the federal funds rate, such as when Apple Inc. borrows money. Sometimes, the additional risk is high and the interest rate on the loan is much higher than the federal funds rate, such as when a loan shark lends money to a gambler.

When the federal funds rate drops, all interest rates typically drop, people borrow more, and more money is created. When the federal funds rate goes up, all interest rates typically go up, people borrow less, and less money is created. How changing interest rates can affect the economy and help in a recession (something you may already be able to anticipate) is the subject of the next chapter.

MONETARY POLICY

How Does the Fed Fight Economic Downturns?

Ever since its founding in 1913, the Fed has described itself as an "independent" agency operated by selfless public servants striving to "fine-tune" the economy through monetary policy. In reality, however, a non-political governmental institution is as likely as a barking cat.

—Thomas DiLorenzo, professor of economics, Loyola University Maryland's Sellinger School of Business

HOW DOES CHANGING THE AMOUNT OF MONEY AFFECT OUR ECONOMY?

Our discussion of inflation made an analogy between the nation's economy and an auction where all of the participants were given a certain number of play "dollars" to buy the goods on display. If the number of play dollars was increased without an increase in the number of goods for sale, people bid and paid more for each good. The change in the financial economy (an increase in the amount of money) affected only the financial economy (it caused inflation)—it did not affect the real economy (the amount of goods for sale).

Now imagine that increasing the number of play dollars caused an increase in the number of goods for sale at the auction. That is precisely what happens when the economy is operating below capacity, such as in a recession, and new money is created. The financial economy impacts the real economy: More money leads to more goods and services. How?

The answer to this question, like the answer to so many of the questions raised in this book, can be found in the realm of psychology. More money makes people more optimistic and hopeful. They focus more on the cash in their wallet and the balance in their bank account and less (actually, not at all) on the distinction made between the financial economy and the real economy in this book. Business owners get optimistic about their ability to earn a profit (some would say their greed kicks in), and they start putting unemployed workers back to work, underutilized factories back in full use, and idle resources back in production. More money floating around encourages consumers to spend on this new production. This, in a nutshell, is how the Fed engages in "monetary policy."

Even though the idea that creating more money creates more economic activity in a recession may be one of the more intuitively obvious parts of this convoluted process, a few examples are useful to really understand what's going on.

If I thought an addition to my house would be nice and the interest rate on a home equity loan (or any loan for that matter) goes down, I am more likely to borrow the money and build that addition. If a company thought of building a new factory and the interest rate on a loan to build it goes down, it's more likely that building project will be profitable and more likely that factory will be built. In both cases, real economic activity increased because interest rates dropped because the Fed incentivized banks to lend out their reserves.

This, however, is just the first round of economic activity due to the newly created money. The homeowner employs an architect, a contractor, and several workers to build the addition who, in turn, spend a good deal of the money that the homeowner pays them. The workers may go out to dinner, buy some extra clothes, take more expensive vacations, or even expand their own homes. Similarly, the company employs all sorts of people to build and eventually operate the factory who, in turn, spend a good deal of the money they are paid on all sorts of things.

Therefore, the new spending enabled by the original bank loan results in further rounds of economic activity. The owner of the restaurant at which the worker on the home addition ate will also see some increase in income and will, in turn, spend at least some of that money. Each successive round of spending is smaller than the preceding round since people do not spend all the money they earn—they save some. Nevertheless, the total increase in spending and economic output can be several times the amount of the original loan. This is another example of the "multiplier" effect we discussed in connection with money earned from exports—the total change in spending is a "multiple" of the initial spending, which in this case was due to the bank loan.

Increased lending leads to increased spending, which leads to increased incomes. And what happens when incomes rise? People invest and spend even more. And what happens when people invest and spend even more? Incomes rise even more. This is the optimistic counterpart to the doom-and-gloom phenomenon discussed in chapter 10 in connection with an economic downturn. In this case, the economy enters a growth phase as spending and incomes rise. To call it an "upward spiral" is an exaggeration, but it's the opposite of the downward spiral of a recession.

Stimulating economic activity in this way is called "expansionary monetary policy." The Fed uses the incentives we discussed in the last chapter to encourage banks to make loans. Banks, therefore, lower interest rates in order to make more loans, thereby stimulating spending and the economy. Most people refer to this complex process simply as "lowering interest rates," since that is the focus of expansionary monetary policy and the mechanism by which economic activity is promoted.*

So why doesn't the Fed keep pumping more and more money into the economy, fueling greater economic activity? This behavior would ensure that they meet one part of their dual mandate: to promote maximum employment. But, as I expect you already know, it would cause them to fail to meet the other part of their dual mandate: stable prices.

At some point, virtually all the people who want jobs and are capable of holding them get them, and the economy is back to operating at full capacity. Will there still be some unemployment? Absolutely. Even in boom times, some people lack the skills to keep a job, are between jobs, or are holding out for a better opportunity. But once the recession has ended and there are at least some opportunities for essentially all people who want and are capable of holding a job, more money and spending would not result in more jobs and output. The economy is operating at full capacity and more money would just bring inflation—the amount of money would be increasing, but the amount of output would not.

In the event the economy is heating up and inflation is gaining steam (too much money chasing too few goods), the Fed can do the reverse of what it does during a recession: It can reduce the money supply. Less money reduces inflation. This action is called "contractionary monetary policy" and is the opposite of expansionary monetary policy. Most people refer to contractionary monetary policy as "raising interest rates" because that is the objective of the policy.

---

* When interest rates are close to zero or, as in certain European countries, drop slightly below zero, the ability to stimulate the economy by lowering interest rates further is no longer an option. Borrowing costs are already so low that there is no room to lower them further to encourage more borrowing. (Interest rates cannot go significantly below zero because if they did, people would stop lending altogether and simply hold their savings in cash.) Economists call this the "zero bound" problem, and it renders monetary policy ineffective in combatting a downturn in the economy.

HOW DOES THE FED DECIDE ON MONETARY POLICY?

When the Fed thinks the economy could use a boost, it employs expansionary monetary policy. How does the Fed know when the economy could use a boost? Sometimes it's clear, such as when the economy is in recession. Many times, it's not as obvious, such as when the economy is doing fine but a downturn looms (or some people think it may loom) on the horizon. The Fed looks at all sorts of data on spending, incomes, changes in inventories, borrowing activity, asset prices, business profits, construction activity, and almost anything that can give a clue as to where the economy is headed.[†]

Despite the sophistication of this process, assessing whether the economy is performing below its true potential or will soon perform below its true potential is really much more of an art than a science. When I was in college, a very long time ago, we learned that any attempt by the Fed to bring the unemployment rate below 6 percent was doomed to cause accelerating inflation. The theory was that since there were too few workers waiting on the sidelines ready to jump into jobs at that point, any attempt to stimulate the economy would require continuous increases in the money supply, resulting in continuous increases in inflation. Nevertheless, before the coronavirus, the unemployment rate had averaged significantly below 6 percent for several years without any sign of increasing inflation. The lesson I've learned is that mathematical models that result in precise numbers may be very useful in the sciences, but are significantly less useful for predicting what drives the economy: human behavior.

The Fed faces similar issues when deciding how much inflation it should tolerate before it tries to cool the economy by engaging in contractionary monetary policy. Its current target is an average

---

† The Federal Open Market Committee of the Fed is responsible for this process. It consists of twelve members—the seven Fed governors, the president of the Federal Reserve Bank of New York, and four of the remaining eleven Reserve Bank presidents, who serve one-year terms on a rotating basis.

of 2 percent annually. Why 2 percent and not 0 percent? Because slowly increasing prices give people a slight nudge to spend money and keep the economy strong. For example, if the price of a new car is expected to go up 2 percent each year rather than stay the same, a few people may be incented to buy the car sooner rather than later. Higher inflation also boosts interest rates, which gives the Fed more room to lower them if needed. Therefore, a small amount of inflation helps the Fed fulfill its goal of maximizing employment, while still keeping prices relatively stable.

Despite the objective-sounding nature of an inflation target of 2 percent per year on average, when the Fed thinks the target will be hit and what they should do about it is very subjective. In other words, if inflation is well below the target, but they think it will start to average more than 2 percent at some point in the near (or not so near) future, they may very well employ contractionary monetary policy—or they may not. If it sounds like the Fed has a lot of discretion and faces a lot of uncertainty as to what it should do, then I've done a good job describing this process.

As recently as 2018, the Fed was engaging in contractionary monetary policy—raising interest rates. Inflation was well below the 2 percent target, but the Fed was concerned that it wouldn't stay that way. Did that fear justify cooling the economy, potentially causing some workers to lose their jobs? How about the effect on the much greater number of workers who didn't lose their jobs? Fewer alternative jobs and a decline in economic activity make it harder for workers to get raises and move up the economic ladder. Is it fair to sacrifice jobs and economic opportunity because the decision makers at the Fed have a mere fear of inflation? If we had believed our professors when they told us that unemployment could not go below 6 percent without accelerating inflation, we might never have pushed unemployment down to 3.5 percent (which is what it was before the coronavirus pandemic), increasing output and providing jobs and opportunity for millions of Americans.

William McChesney Martin, the Fed's chairman during the 1950s and 1960s, commented on the difficulty of deciding how much to lower interest rates to get the economy out of a slump, but not so much that it creates inflation. He said that the Federal Reserve's job is to take away the punch bowl just as the party gets going. As anyone who ever threw a party that got out of hand knows, when to take away the punch bowl is often clear only after it has been out for too long.

The Fed's job of managing the level of economic activity has enormous consequences for every American. Are these judgments being made in the best possible way? Should we, as Congressman Ron Paul of Texas has advocated, "End the Fed"?

END THE FED?

Winston Churchill concluded that democracy is the worst form of government, except for all the others. I think the same can be said of the Federal Reserve System. Hundreds of years of trial and much error have led to where we are today, where the vast majority of nations have delegated control of their money supply to a central bank. We have not abandoned control of this critical function by linking it to the size of a pile of precious metals as we did when we were on the gold standard. We have not delegated it to private sector bankers or, in the case of most virtual currencies, anonymous cyber geeks. Each of those methods would limit our ability as a nation to respond to downturns and save people's jobs and spending power. Those methods may work in some theoretical models, but in the messy real world, they would impose a straitjacket on economic policy and force us to sit idly by as people suffer.

Instead, our government has set up an independent entity, overseen by people who have experience in the fields of economics, finance, and banking. The Fed's control over the money supply (and, consequently, interest rates) has over time reduced the swings in the economic cycle. It has helped curtail economic downturns and the real pain they inflict on many people.

Nevertheless, the judgments as to whether to expand or contract economic activity are made by people who are not representative of society and may be out of touch with the average person. The people selected by the president and confirmed by the Senate as the Fed's governors as well as the much larger group of people who help to decide and implement policy at the Fed and the regional reserve banks are likely to have very different views from most working people. Many Americans struggle to pay their bills, experience job insecurity (since most people don't have fourteen-year job contracts like the Fed governors), and worry about a whole host of events that could push them over the edge financially.

As of this writing, of the four Fed governors (there are three vacancies), three, including the chair, are Republicans, one is a Democrat, and all have held significant high-level positions in the financial industry. Given the choice between risking inflation and causing economic pain for potentially millions of working people by slowing the economy, I wonder whether these people would make the same choices that the average American would make.

Most people pay much less attention to the president's picks for the Fed than his picks for the Supreme Court. The financial industry is the exception in that it closely follows these choices, provides most of the candidates, and maintains close contact with them once they're in office. We need to recognize that the Fed's governors affect our economy just as much as the Supreme Court justices affect our rights as citizens. Therefore, we need to be as vigilant about who is appointed to the Fed as we are about who is appointed to the Supreme Court and, at the risk of stating the obvious, who sits in the White House making those appointments.

We now turn to the other major tool used to fight economic downturns: fiscal policy.

13

FISCAL POLICY

How Can Government Spending and Tax Policies Fight Downturns?

John Maynard Keynes's contribution was not just to advocate spending government money in the middle of a recession. Every government had done that going back to the days of the Irish potato famine. What he gave to us was a way of thinking about the magnitude and the dimensions.

—Paul Samuelson, Nobel Prize–winning economist

WHAT IS THE GOVERNMENT'S ROLE IN FIGHTING A RECESSION?

The Fed's role, as we discussed in the last chapter, is to keep the economy growing and respond to any actual or looming downturn by employing expansionary monetary policy—lowering interest rates and, thereby, encouraging borrowing and spending. In a recession, however, people cut back on spending. Therefore, the lower cost of a loan, just like the lower cost of almost anything during a recession, may not attract new customers. Furthermore, the worse the recession, the less likely lower loan costs will result in new borrowing and spending. What the economy needs is something the Fed cannot offer—a surge of actual spending on goods and services. When consumers won't spend and businesses won't spend, the job of spending and getting the economy moving again falls to the government (Congress and the president).

Prior to the 1930s, however, most economists viewed the economic cycle the way we view the weather: It varies between good and bad, and there's not much we can do to influence it. They believed that markets were "self-correcting" and that in the "long run" a bad economy would find its way back to some kind of normal level of activity. Specifically, they thought a bad economy would eventually cause unemployed workers to keep reducing their wage demands until employers who owned idle factories and workplaces became interested in rehiring them. Even today, there are still some people, although few economists, who oppose government action to help the economy. Their ideas are well summed up by the term "YOYO" economics, which is an acronym for "you're on your own."

Believers in YOYO economics focus on an employer's dropping expenses, but forget about the other side of an employer's ledger. If there's little demand for the employer's products or services, they will not have much interest in ramping up production and hiring new employees regardless of how low wages might drop.

You may be wondering why the early economists failed to recognize that producers won't produce what consumers won't buy. The fact that they were almost exclusively privileged men who enjoyed family wealth or a university faculty position (or both) that sheltered them from the harm that downturns inflicted on most workers is probably why they were mostly blind to this problem. One of them, the economist John Maynard Keynes, broke rank in the early 1930s. He thought the government needed to respond to the real pain many people were enduring as a result of the Great Depression. He took no solace in the prediction that in the long run it would all work out because, as previously quoted, "In the long run, we are all dead."

Doing nothing and just waiting around for a recession to end has major costs in addition to the pain of unemployment and lower incomes. Laid-off workers start to lose their skills, and their chances of going back to their old jobs after the recession ends, diminish. The longer the recession lingers, the greater the chance that they never reenter the job market, particularly if they are older or have spotty work histories. New entrants into the labor force cannot get a start building their skills and being productive. People who enter the labor force in a depressed economy get not only lower wages in their first job, but also lower wages throughout their lives compared to those who enter in a strong economy. Finally, prolonged downturns add fuel to existing social tensions, making people angrier and less willing to work constructively with each other.

The government holds the key to breaking the cycle of decreased spending and dropping incomes. In a recession, when consumers and businesses step back, there is nothing stopping the downward spiral if the government doesn't step forward. The government is essentially the spender of last resort.

How the government should spend in a recession depends on the reason why the economy turned down in the first place. As previously discussed, most downturns, like the Great Depression and the Great Recession of 2008, are due to a "demand shock," a sudden decline in people's spending. Other downturns, like the one brought on by the coronavirus, are due to a "supply shock," a physical impact that reduces the economy's ability to produce. We'll discuss the best government response to each of these shocks separately in the following pages.

HOW SHOULD THE GOVERNMENT RESPOND TO A DEMAND SHOCK RECESSION?

Historians generally credit John Maynard Keynes for coming up with the government remedies for downturns caused by drops in consumer and business spending. His ideas weren't completely original, but like many famous people, he got credit for ideas by popularizing them and getting them implemented in the real world. Keynes advocated that the government increase its spending and/or decrease taxes to get the economy moving again. Government tax and spending policy is called "fiscal policy." Increasing spending and/or decreasing taxes to fight a recession is called a "fiscal policy stimulus" or, more simply, a "stimulus."

Why would this help the economy? Just as every new dollar of spending by the private sector results in a new dollar of income for someone, every new dollar of spending by the government or by an individual who just got a tax cut also results in a new dollar of income for someone. And what happens when people have more income? They spend more. And what happens when they spend even more? They have even more income. (You're an expert on this phenomenon by now.) The economic gloom lifts and the economy enters a new growth phase, in the same way a person can be shaken out of a gloomy mood by a new job with a higher income.

Some of the new spending and/or tax breaks in a recession actually happens automatically, which is great considering how efficiently and constructively Congress tends to react to problems.* Specifically, in a recession, government spending on existing programs like unemployment insurance, food stamps, health insurance subsidies, and other welfare programs increases as more people meet the previously enacted qualifications for receiving benefits under such programs. Also, the amount of tax people owe

---

* Congress's efficiency in responding to economic downturns is summed up in the headline "Fed Chief Sees Decline Over; House Passes Recovery Bill," which appeared in the *New York Times* on March 8, 2002.

goes down as they lose jobs or income. These "automatic stabilizers" may kick in before government officials or others are even aware that the economy has declined. As a result, they help not only those people having a hard time, but also all people, since they aid in stabilizing the whole economy. When those who are suffering economically receive financial assistance, they quickly spend the money, thereby immediately supporting jobs and businesses.

Senator Bernie Sanders and some other politicians have proposed an even more powerful automatic stabilizer: a guaranteed federal job. These federal jobs would grow in number in a recession as people flocked to them, and they would decline as the economy improved and people returned to the private sector. People in these jobs could help repair our aging infrastructure, improve educational opportunities in poor neighborhoods, help with the growing need for elder care, and make America cleaner and greener. This would be so much better than continued unemployment for the people getting these new jobs as well as for our economy. Such a program would likely be expensive, but worrying about the amount of government spending in a recession is like worrying about the water bill when your house is on fire.

How much money the government needs to inject into the economy as a stimulus is a difficult question to answer, even for economists. The reason it's so difficult, as you can guess by now, is that so much in the economy is driven by psychology. The amount of government spending needed to break through the gloom and get people optimistic again is no exception. Try quantifying exactly how many good things would have to happen to get a dispirited friend back to their former self and you'll understand how difficult it is to say precisely how much stimulus is needed to get the economy back on track. The best approach is to spend more, tax less, keep an eye on what's happening in the economy, and adjust as needed.

The reaction to the Great Depression illustrates the difficulty of determining how much stimulus is needed in a downturn. In the 1930s, the government responded to the downturn by spending heavily on New Deal projects—electrifying rural America, upgrading roads, creating art through the Works Progress Administration, and building infrastructure throughout the nation, like the Hoover Dam and the Henry Hudson Parkway. However, the economy never really took off until America's entry into World War II, leading some to the problematic conclusion that war is good for the economy.

The fact is that war is very, very bad for the economy and for the real-live human beings the economy is supposed to serve. War kills people, destroys infrastructure, and diverts production from the things people want to the things they need to win the war. The U.S. economy took off when it entered World War II simply because the threat to countless lives posed by the Nazis lit a fire under the government. It got the government to spend in amounts that would have been unthinkable during peacetime. The weapons of war on which the government spent did not do anything for consumers, but the money earned by the workers employed to make them did. These workers spent the money they earned, thereby increasing incomes and spending and getting the economy back on a path to growth.

Fortunately, in most economic downturns, we do not have a major threat to address like winning a war. So, we have options as to how we should spend stimulus money and/or reduce taxes. These options are the subject of the next two sections.

Stimulus for High Earners Versus Low Earners

Putting money in the pockets of lower-income or unemployed people provides a much more immediate stimulus for the economy than putting money in the pockets of the wealthy. As we have discussed, lower-income people and, in particular, people suffering economic hardship are likely to spend any extra money they get, instantly stimulating the economy. The New Deal projects that employed huge numbers of workers (many of whom had been unemployed) to build parks, roads, and other public facilities are perfect examples of stimulus spending that went right into the economy. The only regret in retrospect about the New Deal projects? They were not big and ambitious enough to put an end to the severe downturn.

In response to the Great Recession of 2008, the government focused most of its hundreds of billions of dollars in stimulus spending on banks and financial institutions rather than on struggling homeowners. If the government had focused the aid on homeowners, a great amount of suffering could have been avoided, both for the homeowners facing eviction and for the communities devastated by vacated homes. Furthermore, spending on homeowners would have helped the government achieve its other goal: saving the financial sector. Instead of funneling cash directly to the banks to ensure their solvency, the government could have funneled the cash to struggling homeowners, thereby eliminating the losses that were causing the banks to hemorrhage money in the first place. Why didn't this happen?

The government officials putting together the aid package were in constant contact with bankers, not struggling homeowners. In fact, many of these officials were either former bankers or aspiring bankers. Few, if any, were struggling homeowners. This is another example of regulatory capture that we discussed in chapter 2. Government officials identify more with the regulated companies than with the general public, with whom they usually have less contact and less in common. The policies they implemented in response to the Great Recession reflected these relationships.

Corporate Bailouts

The one type of stimulus spending that usually receives enthusiastic support from both Democrat and Republican politicians is corporate bailouts. These bailouts involve either giving money or lending money on particularly favorable terms to businesses. The larger the business, the more money it typically gets. The rationale offered for these decisions is that if the airlines go bankrupt, or if the hospitality industry goes bankrupt, or if Boeing goes bankrupt, or if any other major industry goes bankrupt, our economy would be devastated.

Does this make sense? To answer that question, we need to go back to the basic premise of this book: You can use common sense to understand what goes on in the real world. When Delta Airlines gets stimulus money, their planes don't receive the cash. Underutilized planes sit on a tarmac, waiting to go back in service the moment demand for travel returns. Without a bailout, these planes would not sink into the earth or be carted away by departing executives. What might be lost if Delta goes bankrupt due to the absence of a bailout is the management of Delta. Bailout money doesn't save Delta's planes—it saves Delta's executives and shareholders. If Delta went bankrupt, its planes, airport slots, and other assets would simply be sold off and ultimately managed and owned by someone else.

During the coronavirus pandemic, in addition to making a big deal about the planes, the airlines made a big deal about jobs. Specifically, they claimed bailouts enabled them to save jobs. This sounds like a good thing until you question (and you should always question) how much we as taxpayers paid for that "good thing." Airlines received over $50 billion during the pandemic, which means that we paid almost $700,000 for each of the 75,000 jobs the airlines claimed they saved.[1] Therefore, the government could have saved tens of billions of dollars or saved tens of thousands of additional jobs had it directly paid employee wages (as many European nations did) rather than hand the money to corporate management and hope they use it to save some jobs other than their own.

The fallacy of bailouts is true for all companies, including manufacturing companies like Boeing. The factories, equipment, intellectual property, and other valuable assets will not disappear, even if the company doesn't get a cent from the government. What may disappear is the company's current management and shareholders.

You may be concerned that in the absence of a bailout, companies like Delta and Boeing wouldn't maintain their assets and the assets would start to deteriorate. However, since the value of a company's assets is typically many times the cost of simply maintaining them, a decision to not maintain them would be irrational and value destroying. Any company making such a bad decision would sink its long-term potential and, therefore, its share price. If the company's management failed to make the no-brainer decision to spend or borrow to maintain the assets in order to avoid the much greater cost of losing them altogether, there would be no shortage of others who would gladly and profitably make that decision. The company's tanked share price would make it an easy target for a takeover by a company with a sounder approach to valuable assets.

Therefore, in the absence of a bailout, a company may become bankrupt and be bought by a new company. Presumably, the new owner would replace the existing managers. Maybe these new managers would be better than the old ones, or maybe they would be worse (although that's hard to imagine in the case of Boeing—the company that initially advocated keeping their 737 Max in the air despite faulty software that downed two planes, killing a total of 346 people).

The bottom line is that no actual goods or services and none of our nation's productive capacity would be lost if there were no corporate bailouts. Our nation would still have as many airplanes, factories, hotel rooms, and resorts as we do now even if we did not give Delta, Ford, Marriott, and Disney a bailout. We might, however, have different management of those companies.

Without bailouts, well-managed companies are likely to survive and continue to prosper after a recession. Poorly managed ones would be pushed into bankruptcy by the recession and any assets of value would be bought by new owners. The new owners would have the exact same incentives to efficiently provide the goods and services that the old companies had.

Unlike high-level managers who are likely to lose their jobs when a company is taken over, most of the other employees of these companies—the factory workers, the engineers, the accountants, the clerks, and many others—would be unaffected. If they were doing their job well enough to be kept on by the old management during the recession, there is no reason to believe that the new management wouldn't also keep them on, particularly since the new management would be eager for as smooth a transition as possible. Furthermore, better management might improve the company's sales, thereby creating even more jobs than existed under the old management.

The shareholders who own a failing company would, however, likely take a hit because the new owners would almost certainly purchase the failing company at a steep discount. Who are these shareholders? In 2019, the wealthiest 10 percent of American households owned 84 percent of all stocks.[2] Since 2019 and the onset of the coronavirus pandemic, wealth inequality has only increased, further concentrating stock ownership among the wealthiest Americans. Any loss of wealth is unfortunate, but given the suffering caused by an economic downturn, focusing government aid on corporate shareholders is not the most effective or humane use of our money.

Directing the money that would have gone to corporations to Americans who are suffering would provide a more powerful and immediate stimulus. Ironically, doing this would ultimately provide a great benefit to corporate America as well. It would enable consumers to keep buying many of the goods and services those companies produce. We would all be much better off if companies seeking revenue were incented to meet the demands of consumers rather than to cozy up to Washington bureaucrats in a quest for a handout.

Stimulus dollars that simply get handed over to corporate management and their shareholders are stimulus dollars that may not find their way to keeping employees on the payroll or to putting unemployed workers back to work. And employment is what increases the economic pie, unlike adding dollars to a wealthy person's bank account, which just redistributes the pie.

In a recession, we can give cash to those suffering hardship—enabling them to spend and keep the economy afloat—or we can give cash to businesses so that the existing management and shareholders can ride out the hard times. The government faced this tradeoff in the Great Recession and chose to bail out banks rather than homeowners. In essence, we can save the economy from the bottom up or from the top down. Unfortunately, those at the top have more say in this process than those at the bottom.

HOW SHOULD THE GOVERNMENT RESPOND TO A SUPPLY SHOCK RECESSION?

Direct physical harm to a nation, such as damage caused by wars, a pandemic, or a natural catastrophe, that significantly reduces its ability to produce goods and services and results in a recession is mercifully rare. Nevertheless, the coronavirus has made this type of damage and its effects more relevant than ever.

As we discussed, when such supply shocks do happen, they affect people's outlook and, thereby, usually cause a demand shock as well. This one-two punch to the economy results in not only less stuff supplied, but also often less stuff demanded. This situation produces all the bad outcomes associated with a typical demand shock recession (such as unemployment, lower wages, and insolvencies) as well as one additional bad outcome: higher prices for many goods and services. Why does this additional problem arise?

During a demand shock recession, businesses typically lower their prices to try to hang on to customers as incomes and job prospects decline. During a supply shock recession, businesses have less to sell since the nation's productive capacity has been impaired. A war might have destroyed infrastructure, an embargo might lead to an oil or gas shortage, or a pandemic might prevent workers from doing their jobs. Therefore, it becomes more expensive or difficult to produce most goods, resulting in fewer goods produced and higher prices for consumers. The phenomenon of

declining output, coupled with increasing prices, is called "stagfla-
tion," and it was a serious problem following the 1970s surge in oil
prices imposed by OPEC.

The fiscal policy tools (higher government spending and lower
taxes) we discussed in connection with a demand shock recession
are a lot less useful here. In a supply shock recession, the primary
cause of less production isn't that people aren't in the mood to
spend money (even though they aren't after such an event), but
because more production is simply not possible or is too expensive. All of the cheering up in the world will not address the
constraints on production imposed by bombed factories, oil short-
ages, or an infectious disease. In such a situation, putting more
money in people's pockets wouldn't prompt businesses to produce
more stuff because they can't produce more stuff—more money
would just be chasing fewer goods, causing inflation.

Clearly, to remedy the situation, the government must address
the harm that impaired the economy's ability to produce in the
first place. World War II decimated Europe's infrastructure
and, therefore, its economy. The U.S. government's Marshall
Plan provided funds that enabled Europe to rebuild after the
war, and economic growth quickly followed. After the OPEC oil
embargo, the search for new sources of energy took off, leading to a huge increase in domestic oil production as well as the
development of new energy sources. Successfully addressing
the supply problem also addresses any demand problem since
curing the harm that hit the economy usually lifts people's spirits as well.

One of the government's initial responses to the coronavirus,
however, was the biggest corporate bailout in history. As we discussed in connection with demand shocks, corporate bailouts may
be the least effective response to a downturn in the economy.
Most of the cash goes to corporate managers and shareholders—
the people who need money the least and are the least likely to
actually spend it back into the economy. Corporate bailouts are
an even worse response to a supply shock recession since they

divert resources from the critical goal of addressing the event that caused the supply shock in the first place.

In the case of an economic downturn caused by a virus, the best response is to pour money into finding a treatment, cure, or vaccine; get it out to the public; and, in the meantime, provide extensive testing, contact tracing, protective gear, and the like for everyone.[†] Not doing everything possible to address the harm inflicted by a virus prolongs the downturn and all the problems associated with it. Fortunately, although the response to the coronavirus was not perfect, vaccines were quickly developed, which helped the economy to recover. Additionally, the Coronavirus Aid, Relief, and Economic Security Act, also known as the CARES Act, provided extensive support to people who lost income, enabling them to continue spending and limiting the downturn in the economy.

A supply shock is very much like a fire, literally and figuratively. It destroys and demoralizes. The best response is to spare no effort in putting it out as quickly as possible.

PAYING FOR THE RESPONSE

There is a simple reason people and businesses cut back when the economy turns down: They have less money. People are earning and spending less. The same is true for the government. Tax collections fall due to lower incomes. Meanwhile, spending rises due to the automatic stabilizers previously discussed, like food stamps and unemployment insurance. Therefore, one key question remains: Where should the money to pay for the government's new spending or tax cuts come from?

There are only three ways the government can get money: by taxing, borrowing, or creating it. Each is discussed in the following sections.

---

† This assumes such treatment, cure, or vaccine can be developed in a reasonable amount of time. If, however, the supply shock cannot be eliminated, every effort should be made to minimize its effects.

Taxing to Pay for New Government Spending

The government could raise money for new spending by increasing taxes. This, however, would be self-defeating to some extent. To fight a recession, the government needs to significantly increase the total amount of new spending in the economy. New, higher taxes would decrease consumer and business spending, at least partially offsetting the effect of the increased government spending. I said "partially" because, for example, when new taxes fund new wages, workers would likely increase their spending by the full amount of the new wages, but, on the other hand, taxpayers would likely not cut back their spending by the full amount of the new taxes.

High-income taxpayers, however, are less likely to cut back on spending due to a tax increase. Therefore, raising taxes on them to fund an economic stimulus focused on others would result in a significant net positive increase in total spending, boosting the economy. Politicians are, however, reluctant to increase any taxes. This is especially true in a recession and especially true with regard to their top campaign donors who will claim that they will have to cut back on all sorts of spending (including campaign donations) if they have to pay more in tax. Therefore, although higher taxes on the wealthy to fund programs for people in economic distress is a viable way to fund new government spending in a recession, that's not the method our political system choses.

Borrowing to Pay for New Government Spending

Our discussion of government debt in the next chapter will make the distinction between debt incurred for constructive purposes, such as to build infrastructure and educate children, and debt incurred for wasteful purposes, such as to avoid raising taxes and push the bill for current services down the road. Increasing government spending to pull the economy out of a recession is one of the best reasons for borrowing. Avoiding months or years of reduced output, lost wages, and diminished well-being epitomizes a worthy goal. The situation is analogous to an underemployed worker borrowing money to gain new skills, get a better job, and increase their earnings well in excess of the amount borrowed for the training.

Government borrowing in a recession makes sense for another reason. Since there is only a finite amount of money in the economy at any given time, there is only a finite amount of money available to make loans at any given time. When the economy is growing, people, businesses, and the government all compete to borrow those funds. The more the government borrows when the economy is growing, the less there is to borrow for everyone else, such as people who want to start new businesses or grow existing ones. Economists call this the "crowding out" effect. Government borrowing crowds out private borrowing when the economy is growing and businesses are looking to borrow money to grow. The private sector has a harder time finding the funds it needs to finance new factories, equipment, offices, and other capital stock that enlarge or maintain the economy's productive capacity since more funds are going to the government to pay for its deficits.

How does the government lure funds away from private borrowers? It simply offers to pay a higher interest rate than it's currently paying. The higher the interest rate the government pays, the more funds are loaned to the government and the less they are loaned to the private sector.

Which private borrowers get the remaining smaller pot of loans? Those that are able and willing to pay higher interest rates. For example, if Amazon wanted to borrow money to build a new warehouse, there would be no shortage of lenders happy to lend it money at the new higher rate of interest and Amazon would have no trouble paying that new higher rate. However, if someone needed money to open a new restaurant, but had few resources and an uncertain path to profitability, they are much less likely to receive the same reaction from lenders. Even if lenders are available, many such borrowers would be deterred by the higher rates and decide not to borrow. In essence, when the government borrows in good times, some of the money that would have been borrowed by the private sector (most critically to start, expand, and update relatively smaller businesses) is diverted to the government.

When a recession hits, however, businesses and consumers cut back on spending, borrowing drops, and lenders have a difficult time finding creditworthy borrowers. So, when private-sector borrowing drops in a weak economy, government borrowing is just picking up the slack. In a weak economy, government borrowing doesn't crowd out private borrowing. On the contrary, government borrowing enables the government to spend on goods and services, creating jobs and starting the cycle of recovery without shrinking the private sector—the best of both worlds.

Remember that underemployed worker who borrowed to upgrade their skills and got a new job that enabled the payback of the loan with a mere portion of the new, higher earnings? That's what government borrowing in a recession does. Therefore, debt has been the traditional way of funding government deficits in a recession. It enables the government to ramp up spending in a recession without diverting funds from private-sector investment or encountering the political flack it would get from raising taxes.

Creating Money to Pay for New Government Spending

As tempting as it would be to simply create new money to fund government deficits, no major nation today does this. As you may recall, the risk of out-of-control spending and hyperinflation is why our government has delegated control over the money supply to the Fed.

Under our current system, if the government wants to increase spending, it must either persuade voters that a tax increase is justified or persuade investors to buy more government debt. In theory, those constraints impose greater financial discipline on the government. Those constraints also make the cost of new programs transparent since the expense of a new program must be matched by an increase in taxes or government debt. Without that discipline, we run the risk of not just inflation, which in modest amounts is benign, but of runaway spending, hyperinflation, and the collapse of the entire monetary system.

A number of economists, however, believe the government should have the ability to fund programs by creating new money. They call their idea "modern monetary theory," or MMT, and they believe that the government's need to impose taxes or borrow money to fund deficits leads it to spend too timidly. These economists typically support an expansion of government benefits and social programs, to be funded directly by new money. Political leaders such as Bernie Sanders and Alexandria Ocasio-Cortez have supported these ideas.

These economists make the point that I've made throughout this book: New money only causes inflation if it's not matched by new output. Therefore, the government's ability to spend should not be limited by the amount of money it gets by taxing and borrowing (in other words, by the financial economy) as it is under current law. They argue that Congress should give itself the right to create money and only be constricted by the real economy—the nation's actual resources and output. Specifically, if the government creates money to fund programs such as getting unemployed workers back to work, educating children so that they can contribute more as adults, and providing health care to workers so that they take fewer sick days, MMT supporters maintain that the new money will be matched with new output. We could thereby make our nation richer and fairer, while not triggering inflation.

Modern monetary theorists say inflation imposes the only real constraint on what the federal government can spend—not the budget, which can simply be balanced by creating new money. It really is a free lunch if you can create an extra $10 to buy a sandwich and an extra sandwich is added to the nation's economic output as a result. On the other hand, if creating the $10 does not result in adding a new sandwich to the economy, the $10 will cause the price of the existing sandwiches to be bid up. (Remember the auction example where more money chasing the same number of goods leads to higher prices?) These economists therefore advocate creating money to spend on any program where the gain in output would cover the program's cost and, thus, not result in inflation.

In that regard, MMT makes a lot of sense. It's also, notwithstanding its name, not particularly "modern" (remember John Maynard Keynes and our discussion of fiscal policy) or just a mere "theory" (remember our discussion of fiat money and the *fact* that the government can create money out of thin air). Nevertheless, its proponents are probably overly optimistic in thinking that our elected officials would show adequate restraint if they had access to a literally unlimited amount of money. They are also probably overly optimistic in thinking that our elected officials would spend the money they created in ways that would ultimately cause a matching increase in output. There is a major risk that they would waste much of it or simply hand it over to their campaign donors by lowering taxes.

The concern with out-of-control government spending has led to the central banking system we have today, where the Fed, not the politicians, controls the money supply. Given the current state of our politics, this is probably not a good time to experiment with removing constraints on what our elected officials can spend and how much they can cut taxes. What our government *should* do is the subject of the next part of this book.

Part V

THE GOVERNMENT

14

THE NATIONAL DEBT

What Is the Cost of the Government's Unbalanced Budget?

A national debt, if it is not excessive, will be to us a national blessing.

—Alexander Hamilton

GOVERNMENT SPENDING

The total budgets of all levels of government in the United States (the combined federal, state, and local government spending on goods and services, as well as transfers of money to people for them in turn to spend) was estimated at 38.3 percent of GDP in 2019. In most other wealthy nations, the percent of GDP spent by the government is higher.[1] For example, in 2019, 55.3 percent of France's GDP, 49.5 percent of Denmark's GDP, and 44.9 percent of Germany's GDP was spent by their respective governments. These percentage differences may not sound like much until you put them in dollar terms. If the U.S. government were to increase spending by 1 percent of GDP, it would spend another $209 billion, approximately three times the total amount it spent on food stamps in 2019.[2]

The portion of the GDP spent by the public sector versus the private sector is not dictated by natural law or the result of some sophisticated analysis. Like the balance struck between collective versus individual decision making, it's simply the result of the political system. Specifically, it's determined by how much the federal, state, and local governments choose to spend. When you read about Social Security going "bankrupt" or "unaffordable" government programs, that is a political claim, not an economic one. Government always has the *ability* to raise needed funds through taxing and issuing debt—what it may lack is the *will* to raise them.

Since state and local governments cannot create money and, unless Congress takes back the power to create money it gave to the Fed (which it shows no sign of doing), the federal government cannot create money to fund its budget, the constraints on government budgets are very similar to the constraints on people's budgets. Both have an annual income—the government's comes from taxes and an individual's comes from wages and investment income. Both have annual expenditures, which for the government, and for probably too many individuals, exceed income. The amount by which expenditures exceed income (called the budget deficit) is financed by borrowing. Individuals borrow primarily by taking bank loans, credit card advances, or money from family members. Federal, state, and local governments all borrow by issuing debt.

Federal government debt has a variety of names, such as Treasury bonds, notes, bills, and obligations, and it comes in an almost countless variety of forms, in various amounts, with different interest rates, durations, repayment schedules, and other terms and conditions. Nevertheless, it's all just like any other debt—it's money owed by one party (in this case, by the government) to a another (in this case, the person who bought the debt). As previously discussed, people who buy government debt are essentially making a loan to the government, thereby enabling it to run such huge deficits.

Who are these people enabling these deficits by buying government debt? Well, a "thank you" is in order for most readers of this book. If you have ever had a money market account or a bank account, much of that money was invested in U.S. government debt by the financial institution holding your money. In fact, lending money to the government (by purchasing government bonds) is one of the most common uses of bank reserves.

IS THE NATIONAL DEBT A THREAT?

The Amount of Debt

In September 2021, the debt of the federal government (in other words, the amount it owed to others) was approximately $22,300,000,000,000 ($22.3 trillion).[3] That amount is significantly higher than it was before the coronavirus pandemic due to the fall in taxes and extra expenses related to the disease. (For instance, the debt stood at approximately $16.5 trillion in mid-2019 right before the pandemic.) How did our government rack up such a huge bill? What does it mean? Is it a threat to our nation?[*]

In 2021, the U.S. government was expected to spend over $3.6 trillion more than it earned in taxes.[4] That is a record deficit, again primarily due to the coronavirus pandemic. The deficit in future years, however, is expected to be significantly smaller. Nevertheless, during the last several decades (except for a few years during

---

[*] The "total public debt outstanding" for the United States, a number with which people may be more familiar, is closer to $28.4 trillion. While this larger number is technically accurate, it includes over $6 trillion of U.S. government debt held by other branches of the U.S. government. It's money one part of the government owes to another part of the government and, therefore, is not a net obligation the government has to outside parties. It could be completely paid off by merely transferring money from one government account to another government account.

President Clinton's administration), the government has consistently spent more than it earned. That trend is all but certain to continue. For example, in the five years before the pandemic, the budget deficit averaged $690 billion a year. Since the only way to fund deficits is by borrowing, growing deficits means growing debt.

The obvious issue here is whether a debt burden of $22.3 trillion is too much. Although borrowing and owing so much money may seem incomprehensible, if you understand how much debt is okay for you, you can easily understand how much debt is okay for the government. In other words, if each American's share of the debt is reasonable, the total debt of all Americans should be reasonable too.

Clearly, if you or I owed $22.3 trillion, it would be far from okay. But that is not the right comparison. The only way to assess whether someone's debt burden is too onerous is to consider it in relation to their income. What may be ruinous debt for me might seem like pocket change to Jeff Bezos. Therefore, since $22.3 trillion is the total debt of the entire country (all 330 million Americans), we need to know the total income of all Americans. As we previously discussed, the U.S. GDP is approximately $20.9 trillion and, therefore, total incomes are approximately $20.9 trillion.

So, the real issue is whether a debt of $22.3 trillion for an entity with a $20.9 trillion income is too much. These figures are, for most of us, too monumental to get our heads around. To many people, myself included, a billion sounds very much like a trillion and it's hard to appreciate the difference. In particular, I remember a member of Congress mixing up the two when he was discussing a particular expenditure. When asked whether he meant a billion or a trillion dollars, he said he wasn't sure. Could you imagine telling someone about the sandwich you ate for lunch and not being sure whether it cost $10 or $10,000? That's exactly the same magnitude of difference between a billion and a trillion. Therefore, to get a sense of this issue, we must again consider our own finances.

We think about three key facts when assessing someone's debt burden: their income, the amount of their debt, and their interest payments on the debt. We can calculate each of these for each American's share of the national debt to determine if their individual share is reasonable.

First, since we know that the total income for 2020 in the United States was $20.9 trillion and the population was approximately 330 million, we can divide the total income by the total number of people to get the average income per American: roughly $63,333. You may be thinking that seems way too high since the median household in America, which consists of 2.53 people, has an income significantly less than $160,232 (2.53 times the average income per American).[5] And you would be right because the "average" income of $63,333 per American includes all sorts of other benefits that most people's definition of income excludes, such as the benefits that employers pay for that are not included in an employee's taxable income, all the profits that corporations do not distribute to their owners, and many government benefits people receive. In addition, growing income inequality—the concentration of incomes at the top—further distorts this average. For example, when Bill Gates walks into his neighborhood bar, the average income of the bar's patrons soars, but no one becomes any richer and the median income of the patrons is unlikely to change.

Second, since we know that the federal government's total debt is $22.3 trillion, we can divide the total debt by the total number of people to get the debt per person, which is roughly $67,576.

Third, since we know the federal government spent $345 billion on interest payments in 2020, the annual interest payment per American is roughly $1,045 per year.[6]

We can now address whether the national debt is too much by looking at each individual's share of that obligation and their share of the annual interest. So, for a person with $63,333 of economic resources each year, is a total debt of $67,576 with an annual interest payment of $1,045 a year too much?

Your opinion on this is as valid as anyone's, but two points are important to keep in mind when reaching your conclusion. The first is that the typical American has a debt that far exceeds their share of government debt: their mortgage debt. In fact, the typical mortgage loan used to acquire a home far exceeds the borrower's annual income, and we rarely view such borrowing as irresponsible. Additionally, the average American has about $38,000 in personal debt[7] and the average student borrower has about $30,000 in student-loan debt.[8] People ambitious enough to start a business or go to medical school typically have much greater debt obligations. Therefore, $67,576 of debt in this context no longer looks so out of the ordinary.

More importantly than the total amount of debt is how much actually has to be paid each year in interest. That is the real burden on people's finances. An annual interest payment of $1,045 per year (the average American's share of the national debt interest) for a person with $63,333 of economic resources a year may not be pleasant. However, it's certainly not an economically crushing, bankruptcy-inducing, existential problem, like some claim the national debt is. Furthermore, an analysis from the Peterson Institute for International Economics and Lawrence H. Summers of Harvard released in the middle of the coronavirus pandemic estimates that the share of our national budget going to interest payments will be *dropping* in the next several years and will rise only very modestly thereafter.[9]

By looking at the debt on an individual basis, you can see much of the hyperbole surrounding it for what it is. Politically motivated speech can take advantage of most people's inability (like the congressman's) to get their heads around such large numbers, generally with the goal of getting people to agree to slash government spending. The $1,045 in annual interest payments for someone with access to $63,333 a year is simply not a crisis of that magnitude. And, if it's not a crisis for each individual American, it's not a crisis for Americans collectively.

The Reason for the Debt

Whether the debt is a problem or not also depends to a large extent on the reason the debt was incurred in the first place. If a person incurred debt to pay for a particularly extravagant set of vacations or to feed a drug addiction, you could easily conclude that the spending was a waste and a threat to their long-term well-being. How about if the person incurred the debt to buy a home, go to medical school, or start a business? I think your conclusion is likely to be very different.

The same is true of the nation's debt. If the government borrows to grow the economy, such as by funding critical infrastructure, educating children, or pulling us out of a recession, incurring the debt makes sense. In fact, the gain in output could easily be greater than the debt incurred, resulting in an economic home run. It would be analogous to an unemployed person taking out a loan at a 5 percent interest rate to start a business that earns an annual profit of 10 percent, the profit margin of a typical moderately successful business. The previously unemployed person is now earning a living, contributing to the economy, and easily paying off the loan from a portion of the business's profits.

A perfect real-world example of such an investment is a couple of early childhood enrichment programs for disadvantaged children that were analyzed by researchers at the University of Chicago. The investments they reviewed returned 13 percent per year,[10] a return that compares favorably with the vast majority of investment opportunities. Other studies of early childhood intervention programs have also found strong returns.

Unfortunately, however, not all of our government's spending is that wise. If the government incurs debt solely to avoid raising taxes enough to cover routine government expenditures, the debt seems like a bad idea. Instead of today's taxpayers paying for our national defense, health coverage, support for farmers, and other programs, the government has saddled future taxpayers with that burden. (I will take this opportunity as a person above the median age to thank everyone reading this book who is below the median age for subsidizing my government services.)

Similarly, even projects that would otherwise be worthy cannot be justified if the government wastes excessive amounts of money implementing them. For example, New York City recently completed an expansion of its subway system along Second Avenue in Manhattan. The project (construction on which began in 1972) cost $2.5 billion per mile. A very similar project in Paris, a city not exactly known for its low costs, is estimated to cost $450 million a mile.[11] Even the best projects no longer make sense at some bloated price.

As we discussed in chapter 2, the political process ultimately determines what our elected representatives do and what they pay attention to. We need to evaluate those who seek to represent us on not only the policies they say they support, but also their ability to get those policies implemented in an efficient and cost-effective way. To do less risks not only a waste of money, but also further cynicism about our collective ability to make sensible investments in our nation and its people.

Just like private borrowing, some government borrowing enables growth, makes people better off, and, essentially, pays for itself. On the other hand, some borrowing wastes money, leaving only a debt burden in its wake, such as borrowing to subsidize profitable businesses or to fund armaments that the military doesn't even want. The difficulty of distinguishing between the two and the mind-boggling size of the numbers involved make government borrowing a ripe area for politically motivated misleading arguments. I hope you can use the tools in this book to put these issues in perspective and make some sense of them.

WHO PROFITS FROM THE NATIONAL DEBT?

Even if we conclude that a national debt equal to approximately 107 percent of national income is not a danger to our economic well-being, what exactly are the effects of having such a large debt? When, how, and to whom the payments on the national debt are made has consequences. We'll first discuss payments of interest and then repayments of the amount borrowed (the principal).

Interest on the National Debt

As previously discussed, the government's total interest expense for 2020 was $345 billion and each American's individual share of that amount is in the neighborhood of $1,045. That interest payment is funded by taxpayers like you and me. Who gets the interest? The short answer is: Most of it *goes* to taxpayers like you and me. The more detailed answer follows.

As of June 2021, approximately 32 percent of our nation's debt was held by foreigners.[12] That means 68 percent was held by Americans and, therefore, that 68 percent of the interest payments were made to Americans. Even if you don't own any government bonds, part of the money paid by the government as interest on its debt was paid to you as interest on your bank account, as a return on your pension assets, or as interest on your money market fund. The bottom line is that 68 percent of all interest on the national debt is paid by American taxpayers to other Americans.

Does one group of Americans receive an advantage from this transfer? Probably not significantly. Lower-income people hold few government bonds, have little interest income, and have few pension assets, but they also generally pay less in taxes. Higher-income people own more bonds, have more interest-bearing accounts, and have more pension assets, but most (but not all, as we'll see in chapter 16) have relatively higher tax burdens. Therefore, 68 percent of the interest on the debt is paid (through taxes) by more or less the same Americans who receive it. There is no major transfer of wealth going on here.

The 32 percent share of interest payments made to foreigners does transfer spending power from Americans to foreigners. In 2020, this equaled roughly $334 for each American. How bad is parting with $334 of the $63,333 (or 0.53 percent) of goods and services that are produced per person annually in America? Whatever your answer to that question, we can agree that it's hardly the economic crisis it's often made out to be. Even the politicians who complain the loudest about it show little interest in closing the budget deficits that would reduce it.

Who are the foreigners who own American debt? People, businesses, and governments in virtually every nation on earth.[13] We often hear about how much the United States owes to China. Of our total debt outstanding, approximately 4.8 percent of it is held by China. (I would bet you thought that percentage was much higher. And I would bet even more that you did not know that the Japanese and the Europeans *each* hold even more of our debt than the Chinese.) There is something to be said for the Chinese and many of our other potential adversaries having an interest in the success or, at the very least, the continued existence of America and its economy. Furthermore, as we discussed in chapter 6, most of those dollars that go to foreigners come back to the United States as purchases of American-made goods and services.

Repayment of the Debt

That $22.3 trillion of debt is a big number. Nevertheless, just a small portion of this total becomes due each month and is paid off by the government. U.S. debt has always been viewed by investors as one of the safest places to park money, and, therefore, the United States can issue debt at very low interest rates. Our government may seem like any other rich and creditworthy borrower, but it is far superior. Unlike any other borrower, the U.S. government always has the *ability* to pay its obligations—Congress can simply create the money needed to cover the bonds coming due. As you know, that is not how money is created under current law. But Congress has the ability to change the law and put itself in charge of creating money. Less drastically, Congress could always issue new bonds, require the Fed to buy them, and use the proceeds to pay off the old bonds. No other debtor can do either of these things.

Our nation is unusual in that the government is subject to a limit on the total amount of debt it can issue. Since the taxes collected by our government are not sufficient to cover its spending, our government needs to continually issue more debt to make ends meet. Therefore, Congress is regularly required to increase this debt limit. On several occasions, Congress's partisan squabbling almost caused it to miss raising the debt limit in time to prevent the United States from running out of money and defaulting on its obligations. This system in which Congress first approves spending programs and then months or years later has a separate vote on whether to raise the money to actually pay for them is asking for trouble.

In 2011, Standard & Poor's, the debt-rating agency, downgraded the debt of the United States to one notch below its highest and safest rating because of the uncertainty as to whether Congress would get its act together in time to raise the debt limit and avoid a default. (The debt of several other nations, including Germany and Canada, have the highest rating.) The downgrade of U.S. debt is not a statement about our economic situation; it's a statement about our political situation.

Fortunately, as of this writing, U.S. debt is still regarded as a very safe investment and the government is able to issue debt at very low interest rates. This is remarkable considering the downgrade and the continuing threat from many members of Congress that are not willing to allow the government to borrow the money needed to pay for the spending that they previously authorized. At some point, if such uncertainty continues, the interest rate we will have to pay on new debt is likely to increase.

If the deadline for raising the debt limit were actually missed and our government did default, the interest rate on government debt would almost certainly shoot up and funding the government might become difficult. What would happen in such a situation is hard to predict. But to get some sense, think about what would

happen if you ran out of money and stopped paying your bills—
then think about what would happen if most Americans started
doing that as well.

In late 2021, Congress was having what seems to be its usual
debate over whether to approve a needed increase in the debt
limit, and Moody's Analytics assessed the potential consequences
if they failed to act in time.[14] They predicted that if Congress
allowed the United States to default, the results would be "cata-
clysmic." Specifically, they predicted that real GDP would decline
almost 4 percent (over $800 billion), nearly 6 million jobs would
be lost, the unemployment rate would surge to almost 9 percent,
stock prices would drop almost 33 percent (wiping out $15 trillion
in wealth), and all interest rates would spike. They concluded that
"since U.S. Treasury securities no longer would be risk free, future
generations of Americans would pay a steep economic price."

Early in his presidency, Donald Trump had another idea. He
tweeted that America should "start to refinance our debt." Refinancing debt means taking out one or more new loans in order to
pay off one or more old loans before they are due. Refinancing a
loan makes sense when interest rates have dropped since the new
loan would have a lower interest rate (and therefore lower interest
payments) than the old one. Nevertheless, this prudent financial
move is only possible when the old loan at the higher interest
rate specifically allows such repayment before the due date.
Most mortgage loans, the second-largest category of debt after
the national debt, typically allow for early repayment. Therefore,
homeowners often lower their monthly payments when interest
rates drop by refinancing their mortgage loans.

The debt issued by the federal government, however, *cannot*
be refinanced since it simply does not allow for early repayment.
A typical government bond requires the government to pay the
bond's holder a certain amount of interest each year and then
return the principal amount at the end of the bond's term—no
early repayments to reduce the government's interest obligations
are allowed. So, what President Trump proposed would not be

possible. Maybe he was thinking of a situation in which a failing business (say, a casino) is no longer able to pay its debts and works out a deal with its lenders to cut the amount it owes. In this way, the failing business and the lenders avoid the time and expense of fighting over the assets of the company in bankruptcy court. As you can guess, the United States is in a very different position from a failing business, and my sincerest hope is that it stays that way.

Although the United States cannot refinance its existing debt, it does, in essence, refinance the portion of its debt that comes due for repayment each month. You can view the national debt as revolving debt: It's never really paid off because when the old debt comes due, proceeds from newly issued debt cover the cost. The total debt, however, continues to increase because the amount of new debt the government issues is large enough to cover both the old debt being repaid plus the government's ongoing deficit spending. The obvious question is: If the national debt is continuously increasing, is it like a house of cards or a Ponzi scheme that will eventually crumble?

The answer to the question of whether any debt structure will collapse always depends on the amount of income supporting the debt. Mr. Ponzi, like his modern equivalent Bernie Madoff, had no underlying income—he created no value. He simply used new money to pay off old money. When the new money ran low, the inevitable collapse followed. The United States, however, created $20.9 trillion worth of goods and services in 2020 alone and is very likely to create even more in subsequent years.

There are many people who believe that given today's low interest rates and the nation's strong economy, we should be borrowing and spending even more. Paul Krugman, the *New York Times* columnist and Nobel Prize–winning economist, has advocated for a massive infrastructure plan that he believes would cost less than the growth it would add to our economy.

In late 2021, Congress passed the Infrastructure Investment and Jobs Act that provides for approximately $1.2 trillion of spending on "hard" infrastructure, such as transportation projects, high-speed internet access, and environmental improvements. Congress subsequently considered but did not pass an even larger plan that would have increased investments in what many people call human infrastructure: children, education, social programs, and health care. Like hard infrastructure projects, such programs could produce benefits well in excess of their cost.

Unfortunately, many of these wise investments are not made because debt has taken on a bad name. The irony is that many of the politicians who have given it a bad name are the same politicians who are responsible for taking on so much debt in the first place. Paul Ryan, the former speaker of the House of Representatives, spent his career demonizing deficit spending and the debt incurred to finance it. Nevertheless, he was instrumental in helping to pass a huge tax cut in 2017 that the Congressional Budget Office projected would add $1.9 trillion to the government deficit over ten years.[15] He and many others chose to finance tax cuts for the wealthy on the backs of the next generation of taxpayers. This hypocrisy has been and continues to be very costly for our nation and its economic health.

Policies that could improve our nation's economic health are the subject of the next two chapters.

15

GOVERNMENT POLICY AND EARNINGS

How Can Our Economy Become More Equitable and Productive?

A rising tide doesn't raise people who don't have a boat. We have to build the boat for them. We have to give them the basic infrastructure to rise with the tide.

—Rahul Gandhi, member of the Indian Parliament

INCREASING BOTH EQUITY AND PRODUCTIVITY

What can be done to stem the modern economy's march toward greater inequality, less opportunity, and more dissatisfaction? It has been said, "There is a difference between the rich and other people—the rich have more money." (Many people, but not I, take credit for this clever line.) I've quoted this line to make the point that our nation's current level of economic inequality is not something ordained by nature. It's the result of choices we as a society make. We could make different choices that would result in a different allocation of resources and have various other positive and negative consequences (many of which you may be able to anticipate given how much we've covered about our economic system).

In making these choices, we should keep in mind a point made by Senator Elizabeth Warren:

> There is nobody in this country who got rich on their own. Nobody. You built a factory out there—good for you. But I want to be clear. You moved your goods to market on roads the rest of us paid for. You hired workers the rest of us paid to educate. You were safe in your factory because of police forces and fire forces that the rest of us paid for. You didn't have to worry that marauding bands would come and seize everything at your factory. . . . Now look. You built a factory and it turned into something terrific or a great idea—God bless! Keep a hunk of it. But part of the underlying social contract is you take a hunk of that and pay forward for the next kid who comes along.[1]

Whether you're on the left side of the political spectrum (like Senator Warren) or on the right side (like Milton Friedman, the economist whose negative income tax proposal is praised in the next chapter), the best way to determine if a statement makes sense is to evaluate the statement, not who's saying it. And the validity of the point made in the quote above is confirmed by how dependent we all are on the infrastructure set up by previous generations and the skills and efforts of others. Without that, we would be just as likely to have the comforts and security to which we have become accustomed as someone living in the Stone Age. This is a powerful justification for requiring people to give back by paying taxes and for using that money to provide as much opportunity to as many people as possible.

Our goal in these last two chapters is to identify which tax, spending, and other government policies can both decrease income inequality and grow the economic pie by increasing productivity. Why does our goal have two objectives? Because merely shifting around money could easily decrease inequality, but could also reduce work incentives and shrink the economic pie, resulting in less for everyone. Similarly, giving tax breaks for developing labor-saving technology, for example, could boost productivity, but could also increase inequality and all the harms that come with it.

Policies that have the potential to achieve our goal of greater equity and productivity fall into two categories. The first is policies that enable people to earn more money from their work (as well as to have work to start with), which are discussed in this chapter. The second is policies that alter the distribution of income through taxes, spending, and transfers, which are discussed in the next chapter.

GOVERNMENT POLICY AND EARNINGS

The government can help boost people's earnings from work (in other words, the gross income they earn from working before paying taxes or receiving government benefits). How can it do this? Primarily through laws that set minimum wages, government jobs programs, and more support for education and training. Each is discussed in the following pages.

Laws That Boost Earnings

As income inequality has soared, the federal government's policies aimed at boosting wages for people at the lower end of the salary spectrum have barely changed. In fact, the national minimum wage has remained locked at $7.25 per hour for over a decade (although many states and localities have enacted a higher minimum wage). Unions, which also push up wages for workers, have declined in power. Union membership is down to 10.8 percent from 35 percent during the mid-1950s, and private-sector union membership is down to 6.3 percent.[2] So, is there a good reason why we haven't significantly raised the minimum wage or enacted legislation that would strengthen labor's bargaining power? Is the reason solely the political clout of employers?

The answer does, in fact, have a lot to do with the political clout of employers. But even if their clout were overcome, can raising wages through a higher minimum wage or stronger unions be an effective way to mitigate the powerful trends concentrating income at the top? The answer is yes, but only to a limited extent.

Higher wages increase the cost of employees, thereby providing employers with a greater incentive to avoid hiring a U.S. worker by automating the job or outsourcing it to a nation with lower wages. Most economists on the "conservative" side of the political spectrum (and, for many years, most people who taught economics) used this argument to advocate against *any* increase in the minimum wage.

In the real world, however, relatively small increases in the minimum wage have not been associated with any job losses, have successfully put more money in the pockets of low-wage workers, and have actually had a positive effect on the entire local economy due to these workers' increased spending. One noted study looked at the effect of a 1992 minimum-wage increase from $4.25 to $5.05 per hour in New Jersey. Specifically, it analyzed fast-food restaurant employment levels in New Jersey and in neighboring Pennsylvania, which retained the $4.25 per hour minimum wage.[3] It found that employment at fast-food restaurants in New Jersey *increased* by 13 percent relative to similar restaurants in Pennsylvania.

At some point, however, increasing wages through minimum-wage legislation or union pressure would reach a tipping point because of the potential for automating jobs or moving them to nations with lower wages. This is a lesson many Detroit auto workers learned the hard way as auto makers shifted production out of the city in the decades after World War II to take advantage of cheaper labor elsewhere. Clearly, many service jobs, like cleaning and gardening, cannot be automated. But, improving technology will enable more to be, either fully or partially. (Think about the potential effect of self-driving vehicles on the millions of cab, truck, and bus drivers.) Higher wages could accelerate these trends. Even the workers whose jobs cannot be automated could be hurt due to the increased competition from the workers whose jobs were lost to automation.

Furthermore, while not all jobs can be moved abroad to low-wage countries, many can be. For example, according to the American Apparel & Footwear Association, more than 97 percent of apparel and 98 percent of shoes sold in the United States are now made overseas.[4] Many service jobs can also be exported, as a phone call to customer service for many American companies can confirm. This, however, isn't all bad. As previously discussed, outsourcing can provide jobs for people living in extreme poverty in developing countries, help bring nations closer together, and foster international cooperation. But outsourcing does reduce the number of jobs for low-skilled (and some not so low-skilled) workers in America and, therefore, comes at a great cost in terms of our nation's level of economic inequality.

Even when higher wages don't cause workers to lose jobs due to automation or outsourcing, there is the issue of who ultimately pays these higher wages—the owners of the business through reduced profits *or* the business's customers through higher prices. A recent study of McDonald's restaurants found that modest increases in the minimum wage did not result in more labor-saving touch-screen ordering technology, but did result in higher prices for McDonald's customers.[5] When the cost of higher wages is passed on to customers, the benefit of the earnings boost to workers is reduced since they would also face the higher prices. Additionally, the division of income between capital and labor and between the vast majority of workers and those at the very top, our major concerns, is barely affected.

In many cases, however, businesses cannot simply raise their prices to cover the higher wages because they would lose too many customers. Typically, when businesses raise prices, they lose some customers but make more profit from those customers who remain and pay the higher prices. When businesses raise prices to pay for higher wages, there is just a *reduction* in profit for the owner—the higher prices cause them to lose some customers and the extra amount paid by the remaining customers simply covers the higher wage costs.

When the cost of higher wages cannot be passed on to customers, the added expense reduces profitability and can deter the formation of new businesses or bankrupt marginally profitable ones. For example, restauranteurs in New York City, who perennially faulted high rents for pushing them out of business, started citing the increase in the local minimum wage to $15 per hour as the reason for many restaurant failures. Very profitable businesses may just become somewhat less profitable due to the higher minimum wage, but businesses struggling to survive, especially smaller ones, may get pushed out by it. Failing businesses not only hurt their owners and employees, but also result in fewer choices for consumers, fewer jobs, and less of an incentive for the remaining businesses to keep prices low and stay competitive.

Increasing the minimum wage significantly enough to make a major dent in income and wealth inequality would likely take a toll on the total number of jobs and, therefore, the economy in general. Additionally, those with the lowest-paying jobs could be hurt the most by a decline in employment opportunities due to the additional competition for the remaining jobs. Such a situation has the potential to push some workers to accept illegally low wages or some other form of exploitation.

Clearly, modest increases in the minimum wage would avoid most of these problems and put some needed extra money in the pockets of low-wage workers. I am sure you are wondering how high a "modest" increase in the minimum wage might be. So am I. Given economists' track record regarding predictions, I am not confident they could provide an accurate answer. Nevertheless, as with so many issues raised in this book, the real world can provide the answer. The government can raise the minimum wage in gradual steps until these adverse effects start to outweigh the benefits. We have already discussed this kind of "cost-benefit" analysis, something economists *are* especially good at doing.

Fortunately, we have two additional ways to boost earnings that are particularly promising. They are discussed in the following paragraphs.

Government Jobs and Infrastructure

We talked about providing guaranteed government jobs in connection with fighting a recession. There is a good argument to be made that they make sense at all times. Government jobs can boost earnings by increasing competition with the private sector for employees and driving up wages. A guaranteed federal government jobs program would cause whatever wage the government paid (say, $12 per hour or something higher in expensive cities) to become the effective minimum wage—if jobs are available for $12, an employer would have a hard time offering less.

Unlike an increase in the minimum wage, a guaranteed federal jobs program would not decrease the number of jobs. Any worker who lost their job in the private sector due to wage increases would have one waiting for them in the public sector. The program would actually increase employment since many people don't work because they cannot find a job or current wages are an insufficient incentive to get them to take one.

What exactly would people do in these jobs? For starters, they could help make up for the shortfall in our nation's investment in infrastructure. The American Society of Civil Engineers (ASCE) estimates that between 2020 and 2029, the United States will underinvest in our roads, bridges, water systems, and other public facilities by $2.59 trillion.[6] The increase in infrastructure spending planned in 2021 will cover only part of what is needed. The costs of shortchanging our aging infrastructure needs are enormous. For example, the ASCE report notes that the average driver spends $599 per year in extra repairs and operating costs because of poor roadway conditions in urban areas.

A quick look at the public facilities and services (particularly for the very young and the very old) in your area will confirm there is plenty of room for the improvements more federal workers could make possible. In particular, if the government had the staff to provide free or low-cost child care, more parents could enter the labor force and help grow our economy. We should keep in mind that infrastructure doesn't have to be physical. Hiring workers to help provide education, training, or other help to people can improve our well-being just as much as a project involving concrete and steel.

Roosevelt's New Deal provides a good example of what could be accomplished with more federal workers. Almost ninety years later, we're still enjoying and benefitting from the parks, roads, bridges, and other public amenities the New Deal made possible. It would not take much imagination to come up with new projects for improving our nation today. When you add the new projects to the need for maintaining and updating the benefits provided by past generations, there's more than enough work that needs to be done.

In order to build support for such a jobs program, we have to start by overcoming the notion that all government spending is wasteful. Clearly some is and some isn't, just like private-sector spending. Those who think the latter doesn't have its fair share of waste should think about the several hundred billion dollars private insurers and health-care providers spend annually on administration (which, as a percentage of their total spending, is much higher than what government health-care programs spend on administration).[7] Or they could think about the countless billions the private sector spends trying to get people to smoke, drink sugary beverages, or drive some of the least fuel-efficient vehicles. Or they could simply think about the billions of dollars paid to many hedge-fund managers.

For those who still regard government spending as wasteful, the trick to gaining their support might be to focus on the specific improvements to our public amenities and economy that would be possible with a larger federal workforce and, ideally, the reasonable price we would be paying for them. We might just get a different reaction if we do that.

Improving the Workforce

Possibly the most constructive way the government can enable people to earn more is by supporting high-quality education and vocational training—what economists call "human capital." A high level of education and training combined with an effective and reliable government has enabled countries with almost no natural resources, like Switzerland, Japan, and Israel, to become rich. The absence of quality education and training as well as an effective and reliable government has left countries with abundant natural resources, like the Congo, Nigeria, and Venezuela, relatively poor. Nothing better predicts the well-being of a nation, whether measured by wealth, incomes, total output, or simply happiness, than the level of education and skills of its population.

Why is this true? Because investing in people not only benefits them directly, but also enables them to be more productive and create more output. More output per worker is the very definition of a richer nation. And human capital is the most empowering form of capital because, unlike other types, learning and skills cannot be taken or taxed away from those who have it. Acquiring human capital can also create a virtuous cycle where it enables a whole family to improve their lives, become better educated, live more healthfully, and, consequently, contribute even more to the economy. (Better education also helps people identify and support the policies that would improve the economic system and the politicians who are likely to implement them—one of my key goals.) We all need to keep in mind that when educational policy is on the agenda, so much more than educational policy is at stake.

Effectively improving educational outcomes will require both more spending to improve its quality and addressing the legacy of denying many Americans opportunities based on their race and ethnicity. We all benefit when every person is enabled to participate in the economy to the maximum extent of their ability. As we discussed, Americans with the education and skills to compete in international markets have those opportunities and are doing better than ever. Those international markets, however, have hurt many less well-educated or skilled Americans and denied them a role in our economy. Fairness, as well as our own personal economic interests, dictate that we address this inequity and not let human potential go to waste.

Which educational programs provide the greatest benefit is a subject for educational policy analysts. At the very least, as we've discussed, there are various education, health, and nutrition programs for low-income children that provide benefits well beyond their cost. And, at the risk of stating the obvious, programs that enable young people to lead more productive lives and contribute to the economy also reduce the chance that they will become a drain on the economy later in life. Although these programs can eventually pay us back, they will require a significant increase in current funding. This leads us to the other major way the government can mitigate economic inequality: spending and tax policies that focus on income distribution, the subject of the next chapter.

16

TAXES, SPENDING, AND INCOME DISTRIBUTION

What Is the Government's Role in the Distribution of Income?

We can have democracy in this country, or we can have great wealth concentrated in the hands of a few, but we can't have both.

—Louis D. Brandeis, U.S. Supreme Court justice

INCOME REDISTRIBUTION POLICIES

The government has always redistributed incomes (sometimes intentionally and sometimes unintentionally), and the government always has the choice of how much to redistribute—how much to tax, who to tax, how much to spend, and how to spend. Before discussing taxing and spending in detail, we must first discuss one important point that is often overlooked in this context: which level of government offers what.

Americans have the right to live wherever they wish in the United States and wealthy Americans, in particular, are most able to take advantage of that right. If income taxes are too high in one place (for example, New York City has a combined state and city tax rate that can exceed 12 percent of income), they can relocate to another place (for example, Florida has no income tax). Therefore, a locality that tries to redistribute incomes from high earners to low or no earners by significantly increasing income taxes would give an incentive to the high earners to leave and an incentive to low or no earners to come.* In extreme cases, the locality could collect fewer dollars in tax with higher tax rates due to the departure of high earners.

This is particularly true for many municipalities that rely on a relatively small group of taxpayers to fund a relatively large portion of their budget. For example, in 2018, the highest-earning 1 percent of New York City residents paid 43.5 percent of the city's income taxes, 50.5 percent of the city's contribution to New York State income taxes, and more income taxes than the entire lowest-earning 95 percent of city taxpayers.[1] These types of statistics are true for many thriving municipalities.

Changing "residency" to avoid taxes is not as difficult as it may sound. Wealthy people often own multiple homes, and they have some degree of choice as to which one they identify as their "primary residence" or "domicile," which determines where they are subject to income tax. For people who spend less than half the year in one place, changing domiciles may be as simple as filing a "Declaration of Domicile" form. This is exactly what Donald Trump did to shift his primary residence from New York to Florida, thereby lowering his taxes (whatever they may be). The move process could be more complicated for people who wish to spend more than half the year living in the state they wish to "leave" for tax purposes. Nevertheless, the higher the local income tax, the

---

* Documenting the effect an increase in state and local tax rates has on the migration of wealthy residents is very difficult because people move in and out of states for all sorts of reasons (and are typically not questioned as to why they are moving) and the incomes of the wealthy can vary greatly from year to year. Two researchers at Stanford University found that although there is not much evidence that modest tax increases in the range of 1 percent to 3 percent cause migration, larger tax increases "may well have greater salience and impact."[2]

greater the incentive for people who live there to establish a new "primary residence" where the tax is lower or nonexistent.

Leaving the United States to avoid all tax (including the federal income tax, which is much larger than any local government's income tax) is significantly more difficult than merely changing residences within the country. To avoid all federal taxes, a person must formally renounce their U.S. citizenship, hand over their passport, and leave the country. This act would not extinguish liability for any taxes owed prior to relinquishing citizenship or for any future taxes on income earned in the United States, such as income from rental property, Social Security, or pensions. It also limits the amount of time the person can spend back in the States and could render them stateless if they have not already established citizenship elsewhere. Clearly, establishing a new primary residence within the United States is a much easier and less extreme act than renouncing citizenship and surrendering a passport.

State and local governments do have a role in implementing federal policy and experimenting with innovative approaches to helping those in need. Nevertheless, any effort to redistribute income by increasing taxes is likely to be much more successful if done at the national level, where tax bills are high and hard to avoid, than at the local level, where tax bills are lower and easier to avoid. So, we will focus on potential changes in tax and spending policies at the national level.

TAXES

The federal government gets the vast bulk of its money by taxing incomes. In 2020, 85.4 percent of its $3.42 trillion in revenue came from taxes on people's incomes, while 6.2 percent came from taxes on corporations, and the remainder from excise, estate, and other taxes.[3] The federal income tax rate is set by the government and has varied widely over time. As of 2021, the top

U.S. federal income tax rate for individuals is 37 percent.[†] Under President Eisenhower, a 1950s Republican, it was 91 percent (no, that's not a typo). Under President Nixon, also a Republican, it was 70 percent. Under President Obama, a Democrat who was often accused of being a "socialist," it was 35 percent at the beginning of his term and 39.6 percent at the end (again proving the uselessness of such labels).

Similarly, the tax rate on corporate income has varied over time. Under President Trump, the top rate decreased from 35 percent to 21 percent, resulting in greater profitability for corporations, more income for their owners, and higher stock prices. As we discussed in chapter 5, loopholes have allowed most corporations to pay a rate far below this—in many cases, zero.

In order to know the effect any tax has on income inequality, we must first determine whether the tax is progressive, regressive, or flat. Progressive taxes impose *higher* percentage tax rates on taxpayers with higher incomes, thereby making after-tax incomes *more* equal. Regressive taxes impose *lower* percentage tax rates on taxpayers with higher incomes, thereby making after-tax incomes *less* equal. Flat taxes impose the same percentage tax rate on all taxpayers, thereby not affecting income equality.

Most Americans assume that U.S. taxes as a whole are progressive and that high-income people pay a greater portion of their income in taxes than low- or middle-income people. That perception is consistent with the claim Mitt Romney made while running for president in 2012 that "47% of Americans pay no income tax." To Romney, almost half of Americans "are dependent upon government, who believe that they are victims, who believe the government has a responsibility to care for them, who believe that they are entitled to health care, to food, to housing, to you-name-it."[4] His statistic was correct, but his conclusion was wrong.

---

† This is also called the top marginal tax rate and is the tax rate imposed on the last (or highest) dollar of someone's income. This 37 percent rate applies only to income over $518,401 for individuals and to income over $622,051 for married couples filing jointly.

Romney was talking about one particular tax, the "federal income tax." Although this tax raises the most revenue of any single tax imposed in the United States, it's just one of the seemingly countless taxes we pay. For example, we also pay payroll taxes (which fund Social Security and, like the federal income tax, are totally based on incomes), sales taxes, property taxes, gift taxes, transfer taxes, use taxes, tariffs, and many, many others. When taken all together, the other taxes imposed by the federal, state, and local governments (many of which are based on incomes) raise a lot more money than the "federal income tax" Romney was talking about. So, Romney isn't correct in implying that anyone not paying this one particular tax is a deadbeat, since he isn't taking into account all the other taxes they do pay.

Emmanuel Saez and Gabriel Zucman, both of the University of California at Berkeley, did take into account all these other taxes. They looked at the *total* federal, state, and local government taxes paid by each income group in the United States.[5] They found that when *all* taxes are taken into account, most Americans pay between a third and a quarter of their total incomes in taxes. They did, however, also find that the tax rate billionaires paid was not in this range—it was below it. They determined billionaires paid around 23 percent of their total incomes in taxes. Saez and Zucman concluded that the U.S. tax system is basically a flat tax except at the very top, where it becomes regressive. Just how regressive was highlighted by the release of tax data showing how Jeff Bezos, Elon Musk, Michael Bloomberg, and other multibillionaires paid literally nothing in taxes in some recent years and little in most others.[6]

How is it possible that lower-income people pay a higher percentage of their income in taxes than the ultrarich? Although many lower-income people do in fact pay nothing under the "federal income tax" cited by Romney, they are bombarded by many other regressive taxes. For example, since lower-income people spend a larger portion of their income than wealthy people (who, as previously discussed, save and invest more of their income), they wind up paying a greater percentage of their income in sales taxes. The payroll tax that funds Social Security is 12.4 percent of income up to $132,900 (half paid by the employee and half by the employer). It drops to 0 percent on income above that amount, making it regressive. The property tax on a home is equal to a percentage of the home's assessed value. It's calculated without regard to the homeowner's income. Therefore, a higher-income person will pay a smaller percentage of their income in property tax than a lower-income person with a similar house.

When assessing how taxes affect people's disposable incomes (in other words, what they have left to spend after paying all taxes), the *total* tax paid by each person is what's relevant, not how much the person paid in connection with each individual tax. Drawing conclusions about the precise effect of taxes on disposable incomes is challenging given the wide variety of taxes, the difficulty of getting comprehensive data, and their complexity. For instance, the federal income tax code alone has thousands of pages, and the regulations, cases, and commentary interpreting the tax code are many times longer. If we're concerned about income inequality (or, at the very least, having coherent government policies), this system cries out for an overhaul. With that in mind, four major taxes are discussed in the following sections.

The Federal Income Tax

The federal income tax, which was implemented in 1913, is generally viewed as a solidly progressive tax by the vast majority of people who are not tax experts. For the 2020 tax year, a married couple with less than $24,800 in annual income or an individual with less than $12,400 did not owe any federal income tax and did not even need to file a tax return.[7] Individuals with incomes above those amounts did need to complete a tax return and calculate their "taxable income," which is their total income less certain deductions allowed by the tax code. The higher the taxable income, the higher the "tax bracket" or tax rate imposed—the very definition of a progressive tax.

But how progressive is the federal income tax in practice? So much of this book discusses the big picture of what's going on in the economy and tries to avoid unnecessary details. When it comes to taxes, however, the devil really is in the details, and the federal income tax code is one of the best examples of this.

The "taxable income" calculation actually excludes a great deal of income primarily earned by wealthy taxpayers, rendering the federal income tax much less progressive than it seems on the surface. Once taxable income is calculated, the lower capital gains tax rates are applied to the profits made on investments. As you probably recall from chapter 5, the wages earned by workers are almost always taxed at higher rates than the capital gains earned by investors.

I could write a whole book detailing countless other examples of why the federal income tax is less progressive than it seems, but will limit myself to this one paragraph with a few examples. Investment managers, including hedge-fund[‡] executives, are allowed to characterize most of their earnings as capital gains rather than wage income and, thereby, pay a lower tax rate than their secretaries and, for that matter, most taxpayers. Those with the good fortune to inherit money or other assets pay an even lower tax rate (specifically, 0 percent) than those investment managers.[§] Most interest paid on home mortgage loans reduces taxable income, thereby benefitting people who can afford to buy homes over renters and people who can afford to buy more expensive homes over those who can only afford less expensive

---

‡ The term "hedge fund" is generally used to refer to an investment firm that uses more complex or esoteric investment strategies, such as investments in derivative securities, often in conjunction with significant leverage. The original goal of these funds was to offer an alternative, or hedge, against more conventional investments.

§ Inheritance and estate taxes are discussed later in this chapter.

ones. As we discussed, a shareholder does not owe any tax on company profits until they pocket them through a dividend or a sale of their shares, even though they can obtain loans and other benefits based on the greater value of their investment. According to a 2021 White House report, these and many other provisions of the tax code have enabled America's four hundred wealthiest families to pay an average income tax rate of only 8.2 percent for the period from 2010 to 2018.[8]

Contributing to this inequity is a whole industry of well-compensated lawyers and accountants devoted to developing "tax shelters" for the wealthy. Their goal is to help people legally minimize their taxes through various kinds of trusts, offshore investments, and other complex arrangements. Sometimes they slip from tax avoidance, which means legally minimizing a tax bill, into tax evasion, which means illegally cheating the government. This type of illegal activity has become harder to detect, prosecute, and deter due to staff cuts at the Internal Revenue Service.

Natasha Sarin of the University of Pennsylvania Law School and Lawrence H. Summers of Harvard have done extensive research on tax underpayments and enforcement.[9] They estimate that based on current trends, the government will fail to collect $7.5 trillion in taxes that are legally due over a decade and that the top 1 percent of earners is responsible for at least 70 percent of unpaid taxes. Nevertheless, low-income Americans are as likely to be audited as those in the top 1 percent. They further note that only 5 percent of taxpayers earning above $5 million are audited—even though every $1 spent on enforcement would generate more than $11 in greater tax collections.

The harm from allowing more Americans to cheat on their taxes does more than rob the government of revenue—it encourages even more cheating.[10] Social scientists call this phenomenon "behavioral contagion," and it means that people tend to copy other people's behavior. You don't need to be a social scientist, however, to conclude that the more people see others getting away with cheating on their taxes, the more likely those people are to cheat as well.

The bank robber Willie Sutton was once asked why he robbed banks. He replied, "Because that's where the money is." If we want to do something about income inequality, raising taxes on incomes is possibly the most direct, efficient, time-tested way of doing it. All the infrastructure for income taxes is in place. We simply need to increase the rates, eliminate the special lower rates for investment income, and close the loopholes that allow a good deal of income and inheritances to go untaxed.

This is far from a radical proposal. The United States has a long history of higher income tax rates (indeed, as previously noted, these rates have been much higher under some Republican presidents), and the nation prospered nevertheless. For example, during the 1950s, when the top tax rate was 91 percent, the U.S. economy was growing significantly faster than it is today and the middle class was growing in both size and economic well-being. Today's top rate of 37 percent on high incomes can be viewed as relatively modest given that the top rate never dipped below 50 percent between World War II and Ronald Reagan's presidency in the mid-1980s—a four-decade period of massive growth in the American economy.

As I asked way back in chapter 2, would substantially higher tax rates on truly extraordinary earners, such as Mark Zuckerberg, Bill Gates, or Jeff Bezos, have dissuaded them (or a competent alternate) from achieving so much? Similarly, would much higher rates on top incomes cause companies to have trouble finding competent CEOs, studios to have trouble finding stars for major productions, and tech companies to have trouble finding leaders to develop innovative products? Would higher taxes on the top twenty-five hedge-fund managers who earned more than *all* of our nation's kindergarten teachers combined (approximately 158,000 teachers)[11] result in a lack of capable leadership at those hedge funds? Most likely, not.

Furthermore, since many of the top-paying jobs in the United States are in finance, would a tax rate high enough to cause some of the most promising college graduates to reconsider their choice to flock to financial firms really be a bad thing? If existing rates were moderately raised for incomes just over $518,401 (the current threshold for the 37 percent top rate for individuals) and significantly raised for incomes well above that amount (even approaching the 91 percent rate under President Eisenhower), would any harm caused by work disincentives outweigh the benefit in economic equity and a more balanced federal budget? Evidence from the 1950s and some reflection on the behavior of top earners strongly suggest not.

Increasing tax rates on high earners and providing tax exemptions or credits to low earners can make a serious dent in income inequality. Effective ways to mitigate some problems, such as income inequality, are sometimes simpler and nearer at hand than those who prefer the status quo (and their lobbyists) would have us believe.

Wealth Taxes

In the interest of lessening inequality, some nations also impose another tax: a small percentage tax on wealth (the total value of all assets owned by a person, such as real estate, art, stocks, bonds, and businesses). The United States does not have a wealth tax, although virtually every municipality in this country does have a tax on one particular component of people's wealth—a property tax on the assessed value of the real estate a person owns. This means that the value of the most broadly owned major asset, real estate, is annually taxed, but the value of other assets that are more disproportionately owned by the well-off, like stocks, bonds, and other financial assets, are not annually taxed.

Bernie Sanders has proposed imposing a federal wealth tax of 1 percent on a person's net wealth in excess of $32 million that would rise to 8 percent on net wealth in excess of $10 billion. Other politicians such as Elizabeth Warren have similar proposals. The logistics of annually tracking and arriving at an accurate valuation of all the many assets a wealthy person may have (such as shares in private businesses, jewelry, art, and intellectual property) are significant. On the other hand, most wealth-tax proposals (such as Senator Sanders's) kick in at such a high level that only a small fraction of the top 1 percent of households would be subject to it.

Another issue with a wealth tax is that it incentivizes rich people to move at least some of their assets to other nations, where it's more difficult for U.S. authorities to track. Furthermore, taxing the value of a business or farm could cause problems for owners who have their money tied up in the business and lack the cash to pay the tax. Although these difficulties could be overcome, they have discouraged the vast majority of nations from enacting such a tax and have caused several of the few that have enacted it to repeal it. For example, France repealed its wealth tax in 2017 after a government study found that each day at least one millionaire left France and its high tax bills behind to take up residence in a more wealth-friendly nation.[12]

Despite such difficulties, a wealth tax could help reduce economic inequality. Wealth is even less equally distributed than incomes, so such a tax, albeit imperfect, would focus on those with the most resources. For those of us who differ from Mr. Romney and do see our total tax system as favoring the wealthiest, a wealth tax can also help dispel the impression that our tax system is rigged. If people feel the wealthy are paying a fairer share of taxes, it could promote compliance with the tax laws, support for new government programs, and a greater level of satisfaction in general. Perceptions may not matter in physics and biology, but they matter greatly in social sciences like economics.

Inheritance and Estate Taxes

There are two types of taxes that could be imposed upon a person's death. One is an inheritance tax, which is a tax paid by someone who inherits assets. As of this writing, the U.S. government does not have an inheritance tax. Every dollar someone receives as an inheritance is totally untaxed by the federal government (although a few states do impose a tax on inheritances).

Zero tax may sound great for those receiving inheritances, but the reality for them is even better. Assets received through an inheritance and later sold are often subject to lower taxes than assets people buy with their own money. How does that happen? As we discussed, we all pay a capital gains tax on any profit we make when we sell an asset—in other words, on the amount by which the price we sold it for exceeds the price we bought it for. Since a person selling an asset they inherited paid nothing for it, shouldn't the entire sale price be a profit for them? Not according to the tax code. The federal government imposes the capital gains tax only on the increase in value that occurs *after* the inheritance.

An example will help to clarify this significant benefit: Assume you and someone else each bought a stock for $100 ten years ago. This year, that person dies and leaves their stock to their nephew. On the same day as the funeral, both you and the nephew each sell the stock for its current price, which is $1,000. You would owe capital gains tax on $900 (your sale price minus your purchase price). The nephew would owe no tax whatsoever because the tax code only taxes the increase in value since the inheritance. (The nephew inherited the stock and sold it on the same day, all while its value was $1,000.) So, the nephew gets an asset for free, pays no tax when he gets it, and pays a lower tax when he sells it than you paid or that his uncle would have paid had he lived to sell it.

The other tax, the estate tax, is a tax on the total value of the assets of the deceased person and is paid directly out of the estate prior to the distribution of any inheritances. As of 2021, federal law exempted the first $11.7 million of an estate from tax. That exemption is doubled to $23.4 million for a married couple. The Tax Policy Center of the Urban Institute & Brookings Institution estimates that only the richest of the richest Americans (specifically, the top 0.07 percent in 2019) paid *any* estate tax due to these generous exemptions and a wide variety of loopholes.[13]

Between 2018 and 2042, approximately $70 trillion is expected to be handed down through inheritances.[14] New York University law professor Lily Batchelder estimates that the average tax rate on inheritances is 2.1 percent, compared to 15.8 percent on income from work.[15] Furthermore, as we discussed in chapter 2, an estimated 60 percent of all wealth in America is inherited and, unless something changes, that share is likely to keep increasing. Inheritance and estate taxes are, therefore, powerful tools for mitigating the growing role inheritances are playing in concentrating wealth at the top.

Inheritance and estate taxes also have a distinct advantage over almost every other type of tax: They don't discourage any constructive activity. Income taxes can discourage work, sales taxes can discourage the purchase of goods, and property taxes can discourage the development of more and better housing. What might inheritance and estate taxes discourage? Dying?

The bottom line is that people come in only two categories: dead and living. Therefore, lower taxes on the dead mean higher taxes on the living. Clearly, as wealth and incomes become increasingly concentrated at the top, this is an area ripe for reform.

Corporate Income Taxes

The federal government collected $212 billion in 2020 or, as previously mentioned, just 6.2 percent of its total revenue from taxes on corporate profits.[16] The Tax Foundation has estimated that businesses spend over $147 billion annually (in addition to their actual tax payments) filing tax returns and complying with the particularly complicated rules regarding business income taxes.[17] Whether or not their number is accurate, I can confirm from personal experience that tax compliance uses up a great deal of time, effort, and money. The burden is even greater on smaller companies that are less able to afford full-time accountants dedicated to this task as well as tax attorneys skilled at minimizing taxes.

We have already discussed how many large corporations significantly lower their taxes, in many cases to zero, by taking advantage of the tax law's complexity and abundance of loopholes. Therefore, should taxes on corporations be increased? They could be, resulting in greater tax revenue, but also in greater resources devoted to tax compliance and avoidance. Furthermore, to the extent businesses pass on their costs to customers, higher taxes for businesses mean higher prices for the goods and services we buy.

Instead, the government could eliminate all taxes on corporate profits and simply increase taxes on personal investment income enough so that it would cover 100 percent or more of the lost revenue. That way, corporations would save billions; the burden on the IRS would be significantly reduced, saving billions; the distorted incentives caused by the corporate tax code would disappear; the special tax advantages obtained by big-company lobbyists would come to an end; and the United States would become a much simpler and more profitable place to conduct business, thereby creating more jobs and attracting businesses from abroad—all while the U.S. government does not lose any (or actually gains) tax revenue. The wealthy might have to pay a higher tax, but the growth in economic activity and business profitability is likely to more than compensate them for that.

Since this book tries to give an easily understandable overview of our economy, fully discussing this complicated issue would take up too much space and be too much of a diversion. So, why did I bring it up? Eliminating corporate taxation and raising the lost revenue elsewhere is likely to be viewed as a right-wing or "conservative" policy and, therefore, summarily rejected by some readers of this book (the way other readers may have summarily rejected some of the policies I've discussed that are generally viewed as left-wing or "progressive" policies). I, therefore, raised this corporate tax issue to emphasize a key point of this book:

Whether a policy is viewed as a left-wing or right-wing policy should be irrelevant. All that should matter is whether it's a good or bad policy—whether it makes sense, improves the economy, and promotes opportunity. Shifting the burden of corporate tax from the corporation to the investor certainly has the potential to do just that, especially for small businesses. So, like any potentially good policy, it warrants further consideration regardless of where it came from or whatever political label is attached to it.

SPENDING

Prior to the early 1900s, federal government spending was modest and there were no safety net programs. For instance, in the 1930s, the federal government spent 4.9 percent of GDP, whereas in the 2010s it spent 16.4 percent.[18] The last hundred years have seen the government implement a broad range of programs aimed at helping low- and middle-income Americans. In particular, two decades in the twentieth century brought significant increases in such spending. The 1930s brought Social Security (the government's single-largest spending program, which accounts for over $1 trillion in annual spending) and the New Deal programs of President Roosevelt, which vastly increased spending on infrastructure (thereby creating jobs and paychecks) in the wake of the Great Depression. The 1960s brought the "War on Poverty," which included Medicaid (health care for those living in poverty) and Medicare (health care for those over 65 years of age). Together these health programs constitute the government's second-largest source of spending (also over $1 trillion).

In order to give some perspective on federal government spending, in 2019, the year before the coronavirus pandemic affected the budget, the federal government spent a total of $4.4 trillion. Forty-seven percent of that total spending was on Social Security, Medicaid, and Medicare (the programs discussed in the last paragraph), 16 percent on national defense and international security assistance, 8 percent on interest, 8 percent on benefits for federal retirees and veterans, 8 percent on safety net programs (which include unemployment insurance, food stamps, school meals, low-income housing, and child-care assistance), and 13 percent on everything else (which includes transportation infrastructure, science and medical research, and the federal government's contribution to education).[19]

As discussed, some spending, like corporate bailouts and subsidies, increases inequality and does nothing to improve productivity, while other spending, like health-care coverage and education programs, promotes equity and productivity, thereby potentially paying for itself. Rarely mentioned is that much of the spending that would promote equity would directly benefit businesses as well. Since all production relies on two inputs—capital (equipment) and labor—universal health care and better education would improve the quality of labor and, therefore, productivity. No smart businessperson would fail to keep equipment in good shape or allow it to become obsolete. If they don't support the same actions with regard to the labor force—if they don't support ensuring that workers are healthy and have useful skills—then you have to question how smart they really are.

A few politicians have also created proposals for a "universal basic income" (UBI), which would provide a basic income to every citizen with no strings attached. Andrew Yang, who ran in the Democratic primary for president in 2019, proposed a UBI of $12,000 a year for every adult American. This would cost approximately $2.8 trillion a year—which is significantly more than the federal government spends on everything except Social Security, Medicare, and Medicaid.[20] If those three programs were not cut, the government would have no money left for roads, education, research, housing, foreign affairs, law enforcement, or defense, nor any money for a wide range of mandatory expenses (such as payments on its debt and pensions for veterans and federal workers) unless it drastically raised taxes. Even if the government did cut literally every dollar of spending that it was legally entitled to cut, it would still have less than half the money it would need to fund a $12,000 per year UBI.[21]

Mr. Yang did have proposals for an array of new taxes, such as a major new value-added tax, which is a form of sales tax. As previously discussed, sales taxes have typically hit lower-income people harder because they spend a larger portion of their income than wealthier people. Yang also makes assumptions about increased growth, as do most people who advocate for huge new spending programs. Nevertheless, any gain in growth from a UBI would likely be offset by lower growth caused by cutting most other government programs, particularly those that support education, research, and infrastructure. Growth could also be hit because some people might cut back on working due to the guaranteed payment. The bottom line is that the funding for the plan is very unlikely to add up.[22]

Even if it did add up, is sending $12,000 checks to the majority of adults who are doing fine financially a wise way for the government to spend money? Approximately $1.4 trillion of the spending on such a program would go to households earning above the median income. On the other hand, $12,000 checks to adults who are struggling financially would hardly solve their problems, especially in an environment where other government spending has been drastically slashed in order to help fund the UBI. In all fairness to Mr. Yang and UBI proposals in general, the day may come when automation replaces so many jobs that the nation needs a much smaller workforce to produce all the goods and services to which we have become accustomed. UBI programs would make good sense in such an economy where the need for human labor has substantially decreased. In the meantime, concentrating funds on those who need the most help and on where they would have the greatest impact makes the most sense.

One example of a program that targets low and moderate earners is the federal earned income tax credit, which provided almost $63 billion of benefits through the tax system in 2017. To qualify for the tax credit, a person must be employed. In 2020, the credit ranged from $538 to $6,660 and depended primarily on the person's wages and number of dependents. If the tax credit exceeds the amount the person owes in taxes, they receive a check for the excess. Remarkably, this use of federal resources to subsidize low-wage workers and help mitigate some of the effects of income inequality has had support from both Republicans and Democrats. Therefore, an expansion of the credit not only would help these workers, but also might have the benefit of being politically possible.

In the early 1960s, Milton Friedman, an economic advisor to Republican president Ronald Reagan and conservative British prime minister Margaret Thatcher, proposed an even more significant program for directly addressing income inequality. Under Friedman's "negative income tax" proposal, if people had less than a certain level of income, they would get a check from the government rather than pay taxes. The lower their income, the greater their check. The amount of the check would equal a percentage of how far below this income level their earnings were. For example, assume the income level for the program was set at $50,000, and the negative income tax percentage was set at 25 percent. Anyone who earned $30,000 would be below the $50,000 income level by $20,000 and would therefore get a check for $5,000 (which equals 25 percent of the $20,000 shortfall). If a person earned nothing, they would be $50,000 below the cutoff and would therefore get a check for $12,500 (which equals 25 percent of the $50,000 shortfall). And anyone who earned in excess of $50,000 would pay tax as they ordinarily would (and not receive a check from the government as they would under most UBI programs).

The negative income tax is different from UBI programs in that it allocates funds based on need—the more need, the more funds. It's also different from the federal earned income tax credit in that every adult American is eligible, not just those who have a job. Friedman promoted the negative income tax as an administratively simple way to alleviate poverty, while preserving a strong incentive for people to work and contribute to the economy. In the example above, a low-income person would get to keep 75 percent of each extra dollar they earned—a similar percentage to what an upper-middle-income worker gets to keep after taxes and presumably an even more powerful work incentive for people with more limited budgets.

Milton Friedman, who is hugely popular with people who identify as "conservative" despite his plan being viewed as "liberal" by today's standards, further proves that political labels have been so distorted over time that they're practically useless as a description of any coherent set of views. He is also evidence that our politics have shifted since the early 1960s, when he was initially writing. At the risk of stating the obvious, politics greatly affects the ability to address inequality—the subject of the next section.

THE POLITICS OF INCOME DISTRIBUTION

When someone is asked to support a particular policy, the language that's used can bias their response. For example, when people are asked about abortion rights, they may respond differently if they are asked whether they support an unborn baby's right to life, rather than whether they support a woman's right to make choices with regard to her own body. When people are asked about same-sex unions, they may respond differently if they are asked whether they support homosexual marriage, rather than whether they support government interference in a person's choice of a spouse. When people are asked about inheritance taxes, they may respond differently if they are asked whether they support a death tax, rather than whether they support the higher taxes working people will have to pay if rich people can inherit millions of dollars tax free.

This book began by discussing how terms such as "capitalism," "socialism," "communism," and all the other "isms" are so fraught with assumptions and preconceived ideas that using them could actually impede understanding and the ability to assess what policies would work best in the real world. The same is true here for the term "redistribution" of income, and for referring to the process as "taking" income from those who "earned" it and "giving" it to those who didn't. Using these words may cause some people to infer (consciously or unconsciously) that there is something inherently fair, natural, and proper about the way our economy distributes incomes. The more they think income is allocated fairly, the less likely they are to support increasing taxes on some to provide more for others.

This is especially true for most policymakers, who are generally people who succeeded under the current rules, and whose campaign donors definitely succeeded under the current rules. They may, therefore, be predisposed to have a higher regard and respect for the outcomes those rules produce. In particular, they are more likely to attribute their success to their own efforts and less so to the circumstances they encountered in life. Conversely, they are more likely to attribute someone's lack of success to that person's individual failings and less so to the circumstances that person encountered. Successful people may have indeed made good choices, but they often had many good options to choose from.

Economic success is not allocated in proportion to hard work and smarts in some objectively fair, natural process. As we discussed in chapter 2, a person's income is enormously affected by a wide variety of individual factors over which they have little or no control, such as the schools they attend, the neighborhood where they happen to grow up, the resources of their parents, the health care they receive, and, very significantly, luck. What a person earns is also enormously affected by a wide variety of societal factors, such as government policy, the state of the economy when the person enters the job market, the demand for various types of skills, consumer preferences, racial/ethnic/religious/gender biases, and, again very significantly, luck.

Rather than singling out government tax and spending policies as causing a "*re*distribution" of income, we should understand that these government policies are part of the big messy process by which incomes are "distributed" in the first place. For simplicity, I too have used the convention of referring to tax and spending policies as "redistributing" incomes (although I did avoid it in the heading of this section and in the title of this chapter). Nevertheless, support for higher taxes to mitigate income inequality can be subtly undercut by this type of language and the assumptions it incorporates. This is particularly true when these policies are branded by some as "socialist," a word with negative connotations for many. All these loaded references potentially undermine people's ability to objectively assess policies and their effect on them and others.

What someone gets to take home as their earnings at the end of the day is the net result of countless factors. Some of these, such as hard work and smarts, we would likely view as fair. Some, such as family wealth, race, and luck, we would likely view as unfair. And some, such as taxes, we may be on the fence about. But if we are going to make rational and beneficial economic decisions, all these factors need to be seen for what they are: a part of the intricate process resulting in the *distribution* of income.

To use language that downgrades one of them, taxation, as an afterthought designed to "re"do the result of some sanctified process, makes that one effect on incomes seem less legitimate than the others. Only by viewing taxation, and the transfers of income taxation enables, as a valid part of the process by which incomes are determined, can we achieve the goal of this book—to determine the best policies to increase opportunity, grow our economy, and promote faith in our economic system.

EPILOGUE

Now this is not the end. It is not even the beginning of the end.
But it is, perhaps, the end of the beginning.

—Winston Churchill (yet again)

Originally, this book was titled *Economics for Activists*. Its focus
was the people who were troubled by our economic system, yet
optimistic enough to engage in activism in the belief that change
was not only possible, but also that they could play a role in making it happen.

I changed the name to *Understandable Economics* during
the coronavirus crisis. The epidemic further revealed how dys-
functional our economic system had become. The government
extended billions of dollars of assistance to corporations while
many children lacked the internet access needed to continue their
educations. The stock market soared while millions of people lost
jobs. Donald Trump promoted a tax cut focused on the wealthy
while tens of millions of workers lacked access to health care
and diagnostic tests that would determine if they had a disease
that could kill their co-workers and customers. I realized that for

meaningful positive change to occur, support from self-identified activists would not be enough—we would need a much broader group of people to learn about the economic system and work to improve it.

The media's discussion of these issues is often dominated by all sorts of very serious-looking people pontificating on the future of the economy and recommending policy based on their very self-assured predictions. The worst of them dress up their own personal agendas as economic gospel in order to take advantage of most people's lack of economic understanding. Others imply that if you analyze enough data and input it into enough formulas (and have enough media attention), you will get the best solutions.

As we have discussed, making predictions in economics is like making predictions in other social sciences. Both involve forecasting human behavior—a particularly difficult task since what people say, what people think, and what people's actions suggest they are really thinking can be three different things, and each can change with the context. As the economist John Kenneth Galbraith candidly said, "Economists make predictions not because they know, but because they are asked."

Despite the difficulty, we need to make the best judgments we can about the future in order to make it better than the present. At a minimum, this requires some specific knowledge about how systems work, which I hope this book provided, as well as keen observation of the real world, some of which this book provided and most of which I hope you are making and will continue to make on your own.

In 2016, Donald Trump asked potential voters, "What do you have to lose?" The countless people who, over the course of history, perished as economies collapsed and everything from chaos to mass murder ensued could answer that question in a way few Americans alive today can. My hope is that those lost voices are not forgotten—that the deafening noise in our society not drown them out and that they motivate people to understand how the world really works and to put their knowledge to use to improve it.

Whether we continue along our current path or choose a better and fairer one depends on you, the readers of this book. Keep reading, learning, and carefully observing so that you can separate the false rhetoric from what is actually happening in the world. Use what you have learned to become an effective and confident advocate for constructive change. Stand up to those who promote false solutions, support a candidate with great ideas, protest for a cause, or run for elective office yourself. Continued prosperity is unlikely and the loss of so much of what we hold dear is possible if we sit idly by and let those with less insight and understanding call the shots.

NOTES

CHAPTER I

1. Federal Reserve Bank of Dallas. "Time Well Spent, The Declining *Real* Cost of Living in America, 1997 Annual Report, Federal Reserve Bank of Dallas." Accessed December 15, 2021. https://www.dallasfed.org/~/media/documents/fed/annual/1999/ar97.pdf.

2. Worstall, Tim. "The Story of Henry Ford's $5 a Day Wages: It's Not What You Think." *Forbes Magazine*, December 10, 2021. https://www.forbes.com/sites/timworstall/2012/03/04/the-story-of-henry-fords-5-a-day-wages-its-not-what-you-think/#364a6c23766d.

3. Kniesner, Thomas J. "The Full-Time Workweek in the United States, 1900–1970." *Industrial and Labor Relations Review* 30, no. 1 (October 1976). https://doi.org/10.2307/2522747.

4. Organisation for Economic Co-operation and Development ("OECD"). "Average Annual Hours Actually Worked per Worker—OECD Statistics." Accessed December 15, 2021. https://stats.oecd.org/Index.aspx?DataSetCode=ANHRS.

5. U.S. Bureau of Labor Statistics. "Employment by Major Industry Sector." September 8, 2021. https://www.bls.gov/emp/tables/employment-by-major-industry-sector.htm.

6. Amadeo, Kimberly. "What Real GDP per Capita Reveals about Your Lifestyle." *The Balance*, September 17, 2020. https://www.thebalance.com/real-gdp-per-capita-how-to-calculate-data-since-1946-3306028.

Also: Federal Reserve Bank of St. Louis. "Real Gross Domestic Product per Capita." Federal Reserve Economic Data (FRED), November 24, 2021. https://fred.stlouisfed.org/series/A939RX0Q048SBEA.

7. Newport, Frank. "Democrats More Positive about Socialism than Capitalism." Gallup, November 20, 2021. https://news.gallup.com/poll/240725/democrats-positive-socialism-capitalism.aspx.

8. Edelman. "2020 Edelman Trust Barometer." Accessed December 15, 2021. https://www.edelman.com/trust/2020-trust-barometer.

CHAPTER 2

1. See: ChinaFile. "Why Can't China Make Its Food Safe?" *The Atlantic*, May 22, 2013. https://www.theatlantic.com/china/archive/2013/05/why-cant-china-make-its-food-safe/275852/.

Also see: China Labor Watch. "Reports on Labor Conditions in Chinese Factories." May 3, 2021. https://chinalaborwatch.org/reports/.

2. This 60 percent figure is from: Alvaredo, Facundo, et al. "On the share of inheritance in aggregate wealth, Europe and the United States, 1900–2010." Paris School of Economics, October 29, 2015. http://piketty.pse.ens.fr/files/AlvaredoGarbintiPiketty2015.pdf.

Due to data limitations, there are varying estimates of the amount of wealth that is inherited.

See also: Davies, James B., and Anthony E. Shorrocks. "The Distribution of Wealth." *Handbook of Income Distribution*, Volume 1. Elsevier Science B.V., 1999. https://eml.berkeley.edu/~saez/course/Davies,Shorrocks(2000).pdf.

3. Greenstone, Michael, Adam Looney, Jeremy Patashnik, Muxin Yu, and The Hamilton Project. "Thirteen Economic Facts about Social Mobility and the Role of Education." Brookings, November 18, 2016. https://www.brookings.edu/research/thirteen-economic-facts-about-social-mobility-and-the-role-of-education/.

4. Bhutta, Neil, et al. "Disparities in Wealth by Race and Ethnicity in the 2019 Survey of Consumer Finances." Board of Governors of the Federal Reserve System, September 28, 2020. https://www.federalreserve.gov/econres/notes/feds-notes/disparities-in-wealth-by-race-and-ethnicity-in-the-2019-survey-of-consumer-finances-20200928.htm.

5. Poleg, Dror. "The Winners of Remote Work." *New York Times*, August 31, 2021. https://www.nytimes.com/2021/08/31/upshot/remote-work.html?searchResultPosition=1.

6. Federal Reserve Bank of St. Louis. "Gross Domestic Product: Manufacturing (NAICS 31–33) in the United States." FRED, October 1, 2021. https://fred.stlouisfed.org/series/USMANNQGSP. Output is measured in dollars.

7. OECD. "OECD Income (IDD) and Wealth (WDD) Distribution Databases." Accessed December 15, 2021. http://www.oecd.org/social/income-distribution-database.htm.

CHAPTER 3

1. Segal, David. "Going for Broke in Cryptoland." *New York Times*, August 5, 2021. https://www.nytimes.com/2021/08/05/business/hype-coins-cryptocurrency.html.
2. Sharma, Rakesh. "Three People Who Were Supposedly Bitcoin Founder Satoshi Nakamoto." *Investopedia*, September 8, 2021. https://www.investopedia.com/tech/three-people-who-were-supposedly-bitcoin-founder-satoshi-nakamoto/.
3. CoinMarketCap. "All Cryptocurrencies." Accessed December 15, 2021. https://coinmarketcap.com/all/views/all/.
4. Federal Reserve Bank of St. Louis. "Currency in Circulation." Data for November 2021. FRED, December 9, 2021. https://fred.stlouisfed.org/series/CURRCIR.

CHAPTER 4

1. Federal Reserve Bank of St. Louis. "Table 1.1.5. Gross Domestic Product: Annual." FRED. Accessed December 17, 2021. https://fred.stlouisfed.org/release/tables?rid=53&eid=41047.
2. Federal Reserve Bank of St. Louis. "Real Gross Domestic Product." FRED, November 24, 2021. https://fred.stlouisfed.org/series/GDPC1.
3. The Gini index is also known as the Gini coefficient. The only difference is that the latter is expressed on a scale of 0 to 1.
4. All Gini indexes are from: The World Bank. "Gini Index (World Bank Estimate)." Accessed December 17, 2021. https://data.worldbank.org/indicator/SI.POV.GINI.
5. The World Bank. "GDP per Capita (Current US$)." Accessed December 17, 2021. https://data.worldbank.org/indicator/NY.GDP.PCAP.CD.
6. Social Progress Imperative. "Social Progress Index 2021." Accessed December 17, 2021. https://www.socialprogress.org/static/9e62d6c031f30344f34683259839760d/2021%20Social%20Progress%20Index%20Executive%20Summary-compressed_0.pdf.
7. All figures in this paragraph are for 2020 and are from: Bureau of Economic Analysis, U.S. Department of Commerce, "National Income and Product Accounts, Table 1.1.5. Gross Domestic Product." November 24, 2021. https://apps.bea.gov/

iTable/iTable.cfm?reqid=19&step=2#reqid=19&step=2&isuri=1&1921=survey%20and%20are%20for%20the%20First%20Quarter%20of%20 2021.

8. The White House. "Historical Tables, Table 1.1—Summary of Receipts, Outlays, and Surpluses or Deficits (-) as a Percentage of GDP: 1930–2026." Office of Management and Budget. Accessed December 17, 2021. https://www.white house.gov/omb/historical-tables/.

9. Edwards, Chris. "Government Spending Could Top $9 Trillion." Cato Institute, January 26, 2021. https://www.cato.org/blog/government-spending-could-top -9-trillion.

10. Congressional Budget Office. "The Federal Budget in Fiscal Year 2020: An Infographic." April 30, 2021. https://www.cbo.gov/publication/57170.

Also: U.S. Office of Management and Budget. "Budget of the United States Government—Fiscal Year 2022." March 17, 2021. https://www.govinfo.gov/content/ pkg/BUDGET-2022-APP/pdf/BUDGET-2022-APP.pdf.

Also: U.S. Department of Agriculture. "Government Payments by Program, Data Products, Farm Income and Wealth Statistics." Accessed December 17, 2021. https://data.ers.usda.gov/reports.aspx?ID=17833.

CHAPTER 5

1. Manyika, James, et al. "A New Look at the Declining Labor Share of Income in the United States." McKinsey Global Institute, May 2019. https://www .mckinsey.com/~/media/mckinsey/featured%20insights/employment%20and%20 growth/a%20new%20look%20at%20the%20declining%20labor%20share%20 of%20income%20in%20the%20united%20states/mgi-a-new-look-at-the-declining -labor-share-of-income-in-the-united-states.pdf.

2. Federal Reserve Bank of St. Louis. "Gross Domestic Product." FRED, November 24, 2021. https://fred.stlouisfed.org/series/GDP.

Also: U.S. Social Security Administration. "Measures of Central Tendency for Wage Data." Accessed December 15, 2021. https://www.ssa.gov/oact/cola/central .html.

3. Manyika, James, Jan Mischke, Jacques Bughin, Jonathan Woetzel, Mekala Krishnan, and Samuel Cudre. "A New Look at the Declining Labor Share of Income in the United States." McKinsey & Company, May 30, 2019. https:// www.mckinsey.com/featured-insights/employment-and-growth/a-new-look-at-the -declining-labor-share-of-income-in-the-united-states.

Also: Our World in Data. "Labour Share of Gross Domestic Product." Accessed December 15, 2021. https://ourworldindata.org/grapher/labour-share-of -gdp?tab=table.

4. Federal Reserve Bank of St. Louis. "Households and Nonprofit Organizations; Net Worth, Level." FRED, December 9, 2021. https://fred.stlouisfed.org/series/TNWBSHNO. The assets that compose wealth are measured at fair market value.

5. Amazon. "Notice of 2021 Annual Meeting of Shareholders & Proxy Statement." Accessed December 15, 2021. https://s2.q4cdn.com/299287126/files/doc_financials/2021/ar/Amazon-2021-Proxy-Statement.pdf.

6. Gardner, Matthew, Lorena Roque, and Steve Wamhoff. "Corporate Tax Avoidance in the First Year of the Trump Tax Law." Institute on Taxation and Economic Policy, December 16, 2019. https://itep.org/corporate-tax-avoidance-in-the-first-year-of-the-trump-tax-law/.

7. Kent, Ana Hernandez, Lowell Ricketts, and Ray Boshara. "What Wealth Inequality in America Looks Like: Key Facts & Figures." Federal Reserve Bank of St. Louis, August 14, 2019. https://www.stlouisfed.org/open-vault/2019/august/wealth-inequality-in-america-facts-figures?utm_source=Federal%2BReserve%2BBank%2Bof%2BSt.%2BLouis%2BPublications&utm_campaign=ceefe4b9eb-HFSAlert_6-16-2020_COPY_01&utm_medium=email&utm_term=0_c572dedae2-ceefe4b9eb-57450077.

8. Congressional Budget Office. "Trends in Family Wealth, 1989 to 2013." August 18, 2016. https://www.cbo.gov/publication/51846.

CHAPTER 6

1. The World Bank. "GDP (Current US$)." Accessed December 17, 2021. https://data.worldbank.org/indicator/NY.GDP.MKTP.CD?locations=1W.

2. Population Reference Bureau. "PRB's 2020 World Population Data Sheet." October 4, 2021. https://interactives.prb.org/2020-wpds/.

3. Board of Governors of the Federal Reserve System. "How Much Does It Cost to Produce Currency and Coin?" March 9, 2021. https://www.federalreserve.gov/faqs/currency_12771.htm.

4. Board of Governors of the Federal Reserve System. "Currency in Circulation." FRED, December 9, 2021. https://fred.stlouisfed.org/series/CURRCIR.

5. See, for example: Anderson, Richard G., and Marcela M. Williams. "How U.S. Currency Stacks Up—at Home and Abroad." Federal Reserve Bank of St. Louis, Spring 2007.

6. Federal Reserve Bank of St. Louis. "Table 1.1.5. Gross Domestic Product: Annual." FRED. Accessed December 17, 2021. https://fred.stlouisfed.org/release/tables?rid=53&eid=41047.

7. Salary Explorer. "Factory and Manufacturing Average Salaries in India 2021." Accessed December 15, 2021. http://www.salaryexplorer.com/salary-survey.php?loc=100&loctype=1&job=33&jobtype=1.

8. World Population Review. "GDP Ranked by Country 2021." Accessed December 15, 2021. https://worldpopulationreview.com/countries/countries-by -gdp/.

9. See: Bloom, Nicholas, et al. "The Impact of Chinese Trade on U.S. Employment: The Good, The Bad, and The Debatable." July 2019. https://nbloom.people .stanford.edu/sites/g/files/sbiybj4746/f/bhkl_posted_draft.pdf.

See also: Feenstra, Robert C., and Akira Sasahara. "The 'China Shock', Exports and U.S. Employment: A Global Input-Output Analysis." National Bureau of Economic Research, November 20, 2017. https://www.nber.org/papers/w24022.

10. Moody's Analytics. "Trade War Chicken: The Tariffs and the Damage Done." September 2019. https://www.moodysanalytics.com/-/media/article/2019/ trade-war-chicken.pdf.

CHAPTER 7

1. Siblis Research. "Total Market Value of U.S. Stock Market." October 12, 2021. https://siblisresearch.com/data/us-stock-market-value/.

2. Goldman Sachs. "Global Macro Research: Buyback Realities." Issue 77, April 11, 2019. https://www.goldmansachs.com/insights/pages/top-of-mind/buyback -realities/report.pdf.

CHAPTER 8

1. Ross, Stephen A., Randolph Westerfield, and Bradford D. Jordan. *Fundamentals of Corporate Finance*. New York: McGraw Hill, 2012.

2. See: Belanger, Lydia. "Global 500." *Fortune*, May 18, 2020. https://fortune .com/global500/2019/.

See also: Meier, Stephan, and Lea Cassar. "Stop Talking about How CSR Helps Your Bottom Line." *Harvard Business Review*, January 31, 2018. https://hbr.org/2018/01/ stop-talking-about-how-csr-helps-your-bottom-line#:~:text=Today%2C%20 Fortune%20Global%20500%20firms,a%20year%20on%20CSR%20activities.

3. Bureau of Economic Analysis, U.S. Department of Commerce. "Table 14. Gross Domestic Product by Industry Group." Data for 2020. Accessed December 15, 2021. https://www.bea.gov/data/gdp/gdp-industry.

4. Bank for International Settlements. "Explorer: DER. Table D5.1." Accessed December 15, 2021. https://stats.bis.org/statx/srs/tseries/OTC_DERIV/H:A:A:A: 5J:A:5J:A:TO1:TO1:A:A:3:C?t=D5.1&p=20172&x=DER_RISK.3.CL_MARKET_ RISK.T:B:D:A&o=w:19981.,s:line.nn,t:Derivatives%20risk%20category.

5. Pensions & Investments. "80% of Equity Market Cap Held by Institutions." *Pensions & Investments*, April 25, 2017. https://www.pionline.com/article/20170425/INTERACTIVE/170429926/80-of-equity-market-cap-held-by-institutions.

6. U.S. Securities and Exchange Commission. "17 CFR Part 240—Procedural Requirements and Resubmission Thresholds under Exchange Act Rule 14a-8." Accessed December 15, 2021. https://www.sec.gov/rules/final/2020/34-89964.pdf.

7. Tonello, Matteo. "Shareholder Voting in the United States: Trends and Statistics on the 2015–2018 Proxy Season." Harvard Law School Forum on Corporate Governance, November 26, 2018. https://corpgov.law.harvard.edu/2018/11/26/shareholder-voting-in-the-united-states-trends-and-statistics-on-the-2015-2018-proxy-season/.

8. Parker, Ashley, and Philip Rucker. "Trump Taps Kushner to Lead a SWAT Team to Fix Government with Business Ideas." *Washington Post*, March 26, 2017. https://www.washingtonpost.com/politics/trump-taps-kushner-to-lead-a-swat-team-to-fix-government-with-business-ideas/2017/03/26/9714a8b6-1254-11e7-ada0-1489b735b3a3_story.html.

9. Business Roundtable. "One Year Later: Purpose of a Corporation." Accessed December 15, 2021. https://purpose.businessroundtable.org/#:~:text=In%20its%20place%2C%20the%20CEOs,communities%20in%20which%20they%20operate.

10. Zernike, Kate. "Tea Party Set to Win Enough Races for Wide Influence." *New York Times*, October 15, 2010. https://www.nytimes.com/2010/10/15/us/politics/15teaparty.html.

CHAPTER 9

1. Grullon, Gustavo, Yelena Larkin, and Roni Michaely. "Are U.S. Industries Becoming More Concentrated?" June 2016. https://www.cicfconf.org/sites/default/files/paper_388.pdf.

2. Barclays. "Increased Corporate Concentration and the Influence of Market Power." Barclays Impact Series, March 26, 2019. https://www.cib.barclays/content/dam/barclaysmicrosites/ibpublic/documents/our-insights/MarketPower/Barclays-ImpactSeries5-MarketPower_final_2.4MB.pdf.

Also: Wessel, David. "Is Lack of Competition Strangling the U.S. Economy?" *Harvard Business Review*, April 3, 2020. https://hbr.org/2018/03/is-lack-of-competition-strangling-the-u-s-economy.

3. U.S. Small Business Administration. "About S.B.A." Accessed December 15, 2021. https://www.sba.gov/about-sba.

CHAPTER 10

1. Keynes, John Maynard, and Paul R. Krugman. *The General Theory of Employment, Interest, and Money*. Hampshire: Palgrave Macmillan, 2011.

2. Federal Reserve Bank of St. Louis. "All-Transactions House Price Index for the United States." FRED, November 30, 2021. https://fred.stlouisfed.org/series/USSTHPI.

3. Federal Reserve Bank of St. Louis. "Median Household Income in the United States." FRED, September 15, 2021. https://fred.stlouisfed.org/series/MEHOINUSA646N.

4. Federal Reserve Bank of St. Louis. "All-Transactions House Price Index for the United States." FRED, November 30, 2021. https://fred.stlouisfed.org/series/USSTHPI.

CHAPTER 11

1. Galbraith, John Kenneth. *Money: Whence It Came, Where It Went*. Boston: Houghton Mifflin, 1995.

2. Federal Reserve Bank of St. Louis. "M1." FRED, November 23, 2021. https://fred.stlouisfed.org/series/M1SL.

3. Marton, Adam. "Inflation in Hungary after the Second World War." *Hungarian Statistical Review*, Special Number 15. Accessed December 15, 2021. https://www.ksh.hu/statszemle_archive/2012/2012_K15/2012_K15_003.pdf.

4. Federal Reserve Bank of St. Louis. "Assets: Securities Held Outright: Securities Held Outright: Wednesday Level." FRED, December 9, 2021. https://fred.stlouisfed.org/series/WSHOSHO.

5. Davidson, Kate. "Fed Sent $88.5 Billion in Profits to U.S. Treasury in 2020." *Wall Street Journal*, January 11, 2021. https://www.wsj.com/articles/fed-sent-88-5-billion-in-profits-to-u-s-treasury-in-2020-11610384401.

CHAPTER 13

1. Sorkin, Andrew Ross. "Were the Airline Bailouts Really Needed?" *New York Times*, March 16, 2021. https://www.nytimes.com/2021/03/16/business/dealbook/airline-bailouts.html?searchResultPosition=1.

2. Gebeloff, Robert. "Who Owns Stocks? Explaining the Rise in Inequality during the Pandemic." *New York Times*, January 26, 2021. https://www.nytimes.com/2021/01/26/upshot/stocks-pandemic-inequality.html.

Also: Wolff, Edward N. "Household Wealth Trends in the United States, 1962 to 2016: Has Middle Class Wealth Recovered?" National Bureau of Economic Research, November 2017. https://www.nber.org/system/files/working_papers/w24085/w24085.pdf.

CHAPTER 14

1. Organisation for Economic Co-operation and Development. "General Government Spending—OECD Data." Accessed December 15, 2021. https://data.oecd.org/gga/general-government-spending.htm.

2. U.S. Office of Management and Budget. "Budget of the United States Government." March 17, 2021. https://www.govinfo.gov/content/pkg/BUDGET-2021-APP/pdf/BUDGET-2021-APP.pdf.

3. U.S. Department of the Treasury. "Debt to the Penny." U.S. Treasury Fiscal Data. Accessed December 15, 2021. https://fiscaldata.treasury.gov/datasets/debt-to-the-penny/debt-to-the-penny.

4. All figures in this paragraph are from: The White House. "Historical Tables, Table 1.1—Summary of Receipts, Outlays, and Surpluses or Deficits (-) as a Percentage of GDP: 1930–2026." Office of Management and Budget. Accessed December 15, 2021. https://www.whitehouse.gov/omb/historical-tables/.

5. The median household in America in 2020 had 2.53 people (U.S. Census Bureau. "Historical Households Table HH-6. Average Population Per Household and Family: 1940 to Present." November 22, 2021. https://www.census.gov/data/tables/time-series/demo/families/households.html) and an income of $67,521 (Federal Reserve Bank of St. Louis. "Real Median Household Income in the United States." FRED, September 15, 2021. https://fred.stlouisfed.org/series/MEHOINUSA646N).

6. Congressional Budget Office. "Federal Net Interest Costs: A Primer." December 2020. https://www.cbo.gov/publication/56910.

7. Northwestern Mutual Life Insurance Company. "Planning & Progress Study 2018—Depths of Debt." Accessed December 16, 2021. https://news.northwesternmutual.com/planning-and-progress-2018.

8. Student Loan Hero. "A Look at the Shocking Student Loan Debt Statistics for 2021." January 27, 2021. https://studentloanhero.com/student-loan-debt-statistics/.

9. Congressional Budget Office. "Federal Net Interest Costs: A Primer." December 2020. https://www.cbo.gov/publication/56910#_idTextAnchor038.

10. Garcia, Jorge Luis, et al. "Quantifying the Life-cycle Benefits of an Influential Early Childhood Program." February 2019. http://humcap.uchicago.edu/RePEc/hka/wpaper/Garcia_Heckman_Leaf_etal_2016_life-cycle-benefits-ecp_r2.pdf.

11. Rosenthal, Brian M. "The Most Expensive Mile of Subway Track on Earth." *New York Times*, December 29, 2017. https://www.nytimes.com/2017/12/28/nyregion/new-york-subway-construction-costs.html.

12. U.S. Treasury. "Major Holders of Treasury Securities." Accessed December 16, 2021. https://ticdata.treasury.gov/Publish/mfh.txt.

13. Ibid.

14. Zandi, Mark, and Bernard Yaros. "Playing a Dangerous Game with the Debt Limit." Moody's Analytics, September 21, 2021. https://www.moodysanalytics.com/-/media/article/2021/playing-a-dangerous-game-with-the-debt-limit.pdf.

15. U.S. House of Representatives Committee on the Budget. "CBO Confirms GOP Tax Law Contributes to Darkening Fiscal Future." House Budget Committee, April 15, 2020. https://budget.house.gov/publications/report/cbo-confirms-gop-tax-law-contributes-darkening-fiscal-future#:~:text=CBO%20projected%20that%20the%20tax,as%20the%20economy%20grew%20faster.

CHAPTER 15

1. Madison, Lucy. "Elizabeth Warren: 'There Is Nobody in This Country Who Got Rich on His Own.'" CBS News, September 22, 2011. https://www.cbsnews.com/news/elizabeth-warren-there-is-nobody-in-this-country-who-got-rich-on-his-own/.

2. U.S. Bureau of Labor Statistics. "Union Members Summary." January 22, 2021. https://www.bls.gov/news.release/union2.nr0.htm.

Also: Greenhouse, Steven. "Union Membership in U.S. Fell to a 70-Year Low Last Year." *New York Times*, January 21, 2011. https://www.nytimes.com/2011/01/22/business/22union.html.

3. Card, David, and Alan B. Krueger. "Minimum Wages and Employment: A Case Study of the Fast Food Industry in New Jersey and Pennsylvania." National Bureau of Economic Research, October 1, 1993. https://www.nber.org/papers/w4509#:~:text=David%20Card%2C%20Alan%20B.,Krueger&text=On%20April%201%2C%201992%20New,the%20rise%20in%20the%20minimum.

4. Wee, Heesun. "'Made in USA' Fuels New Manufacturing Hubs in Apparel." CNBC, September 23, 2013. https://www.cnbc.com/2013/09/23/inside-made-in-the-usa-showcasing-skilled-garment-workers.html#:~:text=More%20than%2097%20percent%20of,the%20U.S.%20was%20made%20domestically.

5. Ashenfelter, Orley, and Štěpán Jurajda. "Wages, Minimum Wages, and Price Pass-Through: The Case of McDonald's Restaurants." Working paper, Princeton University, January 2021. https://dataspace.princeton.edu/bitstream/88435/dsp01sb397c318/4/646.pdf.

6. American Society of Civil Engineers. "Investment Gap 2020–2029: ASCE's 2021 Infrastructure Report Card." July 19, 2021. https://infrastructurereportcard .org/resources/investment-gap-2020-2029/.

7. Carroll, Linda. "More than a Third of U.S. Healthcare Costs Go to Bureaucracy." Thomson Reuters, January 6, 2020. https://www.reuters.com/ article/us-health-costs-administration/more-than-a-third-of-u-s-healthcare-costs-go -to-bureaucracy-idUSKBN1Z5261.

Also: Frakt, Austin. "Is Medicare for All the Answer to Sky-High Administrative Costs?" *New York Times*, October 15, 2018. https://www.nytimes.com/2018/10/15/ upshot/is-medicare-for-all-the-answer-to-sky-high-administrative-costs.html.

CHAPTER 16

1. McMahon, E. J. "NYC's High-Income Tax Habit." Empire Center for Public Policy, October 25, 2018. https://www.empirecenter.org/publications/nycs-high -income-tax-habit/.

2. Young, Cristobal, and Charles Varner. "Do Millionaires Migrate When Tax Rates Are Raised?" *Stanford University Pathways*, Summer 2014. https://inequal ity.stanford.edu/sites/default/files/media/_media/pdf/pathways/summer_2014/Path ways_Summer_2014_YoungVarner.pdf.

3. U.S. Congressional Budget Office. "Revenues in Fiscal Year 2020: An Info-graphic." April 30, 2021. https://www.cbo.gov/publication/57173.

4. Madison, Lucy. "Fact-Checking Romney's '47 Percent' Comment." CBS News, September 25, 2012. https://www.cbsnews.com/news/fact-checking-romneys -47-percent-comment/.

5. Saez, Emmanuel, and Gabriel Zucman. *The Triumph of Injustice: How the Rich Dodge Taxes and How to Make Them Pay*. New York: W. W. Norton, 2020.

6. Eisinger, Jesse, Jeff Ernsthausen, and Paul Kiel. "The Secret IRS Files: Trove of Never-before-Seen Records Reveal How the Wealthiest Avoid Income Tax." ProPublica. Accessed December 16, 2021. https://www.propublica.org/article/ the-secret-irs-files-trove-of-never-before-seen-records-reveal-how-the-wealthiest -avoid-income-tax.

7. U.S. Internal Revenue Service. "IRS Provides Tax Inflation Adjustments for Tax Year 2020." November 6, 2019. https://www.irs.gov/newsroom/irs-provides-tax -inflation-adjustments-for-tax-year-2020#:~:text=For%20single%20taxpayers%20 and%20married,tax%20year%202020%2C%20up%20%24300.

8. Leiserson, Greg, and Danny Yagan. "What Is the Average Federal Individual Income Tax Rate on the Wealthiest Americans?" *The White House Blog*, Novem-ber 30, 2021. https://www.whitehouse.gov/cea/blog/2021/09/23/what-is-the-average -federal-individual-income-tax-rate-on-the-wealthiest-americans/.

9. All the statistics in this paragraph come from:
Sarin, Natasha. "The I.R.S. Is Outgunned." *New York Times*, October 2, 2020. https://www.nytimes.com/2020/10/02/opinion/sunday/irs-tax-income-inequality .html. And: Summers, Lawrence H., and Natasha Sarin. "Opinion: Yes, Our Tax System Needs Reform. Let's Start with This First Step." *Washington Post*, November 22, 2019. https://www.washingtonpost.com/opinions/yes-our-tax-system -needs-reform-lets-start-with-this-first-step/2019/11/17/4d23f8d4-07dd-11ea-924a -28d87132c7ec_story.html.

10. Frank, Robert H. "Without More Enforcement, Tax Evasion Will Spread Like a Virus." *New York Times*, October 30, 2020. https://www.nytimes.com/2020/10/30/ business/tax-evasion-virus-IRS.html?searchResultPosition=3.

11. Bump, Philip. "The 25 Top Hedge Fund Managers Earn More than All Kindergarten Teachers Combined." *Washington Post*, November 25, 2021. https:// www.washingtonpost.com/news/the-fix/wp/2015/05/12/the-top-25-hedge-fund -managers-earn-more-than-all-kindergarten-teachers-combined/.

12. Moore, Molly. "Old Money, New Money Flee France and Its Wealth Tax." *Washington Post*, July 16, 2006. https://www.washingtonpost.com/archive/politics/ 2006/07/16/old-money-new-money-flee-france-and-its-wealth-tax/49ac2ec7-c1b2 -423e-a89b-699750275cd4/.

13. Tax Policy Center of the Urban Institute & Brookings Institution. "How Many People Pay the Estate Tax?" Accessed December 16, 2021. https://www.tax policycenter.org/briefing-book/how-many-people-pay-estate-tax.

14. Eisen, Ben, and Anne Tergesen. "Older Americans Stockpiled a Record $35 Trillion. The Time Has Come to Give It Away." *Wall Street Journal*, July 2, 2021. https://www.wsj.com/articles/older-americans-35-trillion-wealth-giving-away-heirs -philanthropy-11625234216.

15. Batchelder, Lily. "Leveling the Playing Field between Inherited Income and Income from Work through an Inheritance Tax." New York University School of Law. Accessed December 16, 2021. https://www.hamiltonproject.org/assets/files/ Batchelder_LO_FINAL.pdf.

16. Congressional Budget Office. "Revenues in Fiscal Year 2020: An Info- graphic." April 30, 2021. https://www.cbo.gov/publication/57173.

17. Hodge, Scott A. "The Compliance Costs of IRS Regulations." Tax Founda- tion, June 15, 2020. https://taxfoundation.org/compliance-costs-irs-regulations/.

18. The White House. "Historical Tables, Table 1.2—Summary of Receipts, Outlays, and Surpluses or Deficits (-) as a Percentage of GDP: 1930–2026." Office of Management and Budget. Accessed December 17, 2021. https://www.white house.gov/omb/historical-tables/.

19. Congressional Budget Office. "The Federal Budget in 2019: An Info- graphic." April 15, 2020. https://www.cbo.gov/publication/56324.

20. Center on Budget and Policy Priorities. "Policy Basics: Where Do Our Fed- eral Tax Dollars Go?" April 9, 2020. https://www.cbpp.org/research/federal-budget/ policy-basics-where-do-our-federal-tax-dollars-go.

21. Tax Policy Center of the Urban Institute & Brookings Institution. "How Does the Federal Government Spend Its Money?" Accessed December 16, 2021. https://www.taxpolicycenter.org/briefing-book/how-does-federal-government -spend-its-money#:~:text=How%20does%20the%20federal%20government%20 spend%20its%20money%3F,totaled%20%244.4%20trillion%20in%202019.

22. Pomerleau, Kyle. "Does Andrew Yang's 'Freedom Dividend' Proposal Add Up?" Tax Foundation, January 2, 2020. https://taxfoundation.org/andrew-yang -value-added-tax-universal-basic-income/.

ACKNOWLEDGMENTS

There are countless people who have made this book possible by either contributing ideas, helping me to better understand how our economy works, or simply listening to my incessant tirades about the economy and (through their expressions) forcing me to be more succinct and coherent. They range from co-workers at my father's Met Foods Store in Brooklyn to students at NYU and the Lander College for Men. I have been fortunate to know so many interesting and helpful people in my life, and I could not be more grateful for that.

There are a few people who directly helped to create this book. Grace Layer meticulously edited multiple drafts of the manuscript, and without her help this book would not have been possible. Grace is a true editing prodigy. Michael Goodwin, the author of *Economix*, also went through the manuscript word by word and helped me make my points more balanced and compelling. David Berman, my spouse, carefully reviewed the entire manuscript. As helpful as his comments were, our countless discussions of many of the ideas in the book were indispensable in enabling me to put them into written form. Antoine Martin of the Federal Reserve

Bank of New York reviewed the sections of the book regarding the Fed and provided many essential comments on its operations. Finally, my editor, Jake Bonar of Prometheus Books, could not have been more helpful. He was the last to review the manuscript and still managed to find many ways to improve it.

This book would not have been published without the efforts of my agent, Susan Schulman. I am deeply indebted to her for taking on a book by a first-time author on a subject that is not known for its marketability. I also thank Linda Migalti, her rights director, for handling the audio and foreign rights.

Several friends also helped to make this book possible. Sari Locker helped turn my ideas into a formal proposal, and without it I would not have had the benefit of Susan's representation. Becky Givan provided critical information and advice about publishing at the beginning of this process, when I needed it most. Ryan Senser helped me brainstorm ideas that resulted in the final title and subtitle. I am thankful to them and to all my other friends and family who provided so much support and encouragement.

INDEX